THE WISDOM OF JESUS BEN SIRACH

(Sinai ar. 155. IXth / Xth cent.)

CORPUS

SCRIPTORUM CHRISTIANORUM ORIENTALIUM

EDITUM CONSILIO

UNIVERSITATIS CATHOLICAE AMERICAE

ET UNIVERSITATIS CATHOLICAE LOVANIENSIS

Vol. 358

SCRIPTORES ARABICI

TOMUS 31

THE WISDOM OF JESUS BEN SIRACH

(Sinai ar. 155. IXth / Xth cent.)

TRANSLATED

BY

RICHARD M. FRANK

LOUVAIN

SECRÉTARIAT DU CorpusSCO

WAVERSEBAAN, 49

1974

Imprimerie Orientaliste, s.p.r.l., Louvain (Belgique)

D/1974/0602/4

INTRODUCTION

Concerning the basic content and order of the Book of *Sirach* one needs no introduction here. On the other hand, while it would require far too much space to give here an adequate account of the techniques and stylistic peculiarities of the Arabic translation, it would be well to make a few remarks on one aspect of the character and tone of the version since it is of special interest and, most importantly to the present purpose, has effectively influenced the basic orientation of the English translation and determined the manner in which a number of elements have been handled.

Generally, the translation is quite « Arabic. » That is, although stylistically the work does not, by any means, come up to the standards of good literary Arabic, the translator has made a consistent effort to avoid the infelicities and barbarisms of « translation Arabic » and to produce a work that could, to some extent, stand on its own merits and be read with profit by those who did not necessarily have a knowledge of the Bible or an ear trained to the overtones of Jewish or Christian religious language. The translation is, thus, never slavish but quite on the contrary tends to be quite free, often to the point of rather free paraphrasing, though seldom is the original sense completely lost or given up. Its most striking feature, however, is that it has throughout a clear and unambiguous Muslim cast that is clearly not the result of later editing but belongs to the original translation.

This tone is effected in part and most frequently by the consistent use of terms which, though not, perhaps, exclusively Islamic, are nonetheless, within the context, thoroughly Muslim in their resonance. To cite several of the most common and obvious examples, we find *faqîh* used (though not exclusively) throughout the text to render Greek συνετός, and likewise *munâfiq* for ἄνομος, *ǧaḥîm* for ᾅδης, *sunna* for νόμος, and, more significantly, *mu'min* for εὐσεβής and *kâfir* for ἀσεβής.[1] The use of such « Muslim » terms is, to be sure, hardly unknown in early Arabic translations of the Bible,[2] but the

---

[1] For citations, see the *Index of Correspondences* following the text.

[2] Some such usage is found, for example, in the translation of Jeremiah done by Pethion b. Ayyûb as-Sahhâr (cf. *CBQ* 21 [1959] 139 ff) but it is to be noted that neither there nor in his translations of the minor prophets (I have not examined his other works)

most common practice in such translations is quite different.[3] Again, we find a number of instances in which the wording of the Arabic has a somewhat koranic ring, as for example in 2.11 where رؤف رحيم stands for οἰκτρκίμων or in 15.18 where we find ἰσχυρός rendered by ‌وهو الجبار القوى.

Of itself, none of these things is sufficient to indicate that the translator deliberately wished to islamicise the book. Individual words and turns of phrase need not be exclusively and necessarily Islamic apart from all considerations of context and overall usage. Allowing the tendency to double many adjectives for stylistic reasons, one notes that most cases of quasi-koranic phrasing prove, upon examination, to be, in fact, the simplest and most felicitous way of reproducing the original sense in Arabic. Significantly too it should be noted that the basic vocabulary of the *Koran* had, undoubtedly, a clear religious resonance that the *Koran* employed but did not in all cases originate.

There are, however, quite unambiguous evidences in this version of *Sirach* that the translator either intended his work for a Muslim audience or at least wished to make it acceptable to Muslim readers in both style and content. This is manifest in a number of places where material that might be considered in disaccord with orthodox Muslim belief or practice has been either paraphrased or suppressed outright. One or two obvious examples will suffice here to illustrate what has been done.

The most remarkable instance is found in the rendering of 15.14 where in place of αὐτὸς ἐξ ἀρχῆς ἐποίησεν ἄνθρωπον καὶ ἀφῆκεν αὐτὸν ἐν χειρὶ διαβουλίου αὐτοῦ we read وانه هو الذى خلق الانسان فى البدئ ثم امره ونهاه. It is conceivable, of course, that the pronoun αὐτοῦ, against the rather obvious sense of the verse, was taken to refer to God and that we have, therefore, to do with a free paraphrase; but on the other hand, the Muslim tone of the whole verse and especially of the phrase « He commanded him and forbade him » is unavoidably clear. The final rendering is, in fact, surprisingly similar to a

---

does one find any parallel to the truly Muslim adaptations that occur in the present version of *Sirach*; cf. *infra*.

[3] The usage of the *Sirach* differs completely from that of the Pauline Epistles which follow in the same manuscript (published by M. GIBSON in *Studia Sinaitica* II, London, 1894), where the translation, in accord with the normal pattern of such things, follows the original text most slavishly.

line in the *Fiqh al-Akbar* II where we read خلق الله تعالى الخلاق سليا

من الكفر والايمان ثم خاطبهم وامرهم ونهاهم.[4] Evidently what we have

here is a careful avoidance of a phrase that, in its original form, raised,
in a rather radical way, the question of man's free determination and
creation of his acts, a subject which was under fierce and partisan
debate among various schools of Muslim thought from a quite early
date. The substitution in the translation, like the phrase of *al-Fiqh
al-Akbar* II, neatly suppresses the contention in taking a middle
ground between the *qadarîya* and the *ğabrîya*.[5] Thus also, it is most
probable that 11.16a ($\pi\lambda\acute{a}\nu\eta$ $\kappa a\grave{\iota}$ $\sigma\kappa\acute{o}\tau os$ $\dot{a}\mu a\rho\tau o\lambda o\hat{\iota} s$ $\sigma v\nu\acute{e}\kappa\tau\iota\sigma\tau a\iota.$), in
the context of the preceding hemistisch, was dropped because of the
implication of a creative agency other than God's. The paraphrasing
of 16.28b (... $o\dot{v}\kappa$ $\dot{a}\pi\epsilon\iota\theta\acute{\eta}\sigma ov\sigma\iota$ $\tau o\hat{v}$ $\acute{\rho}\acute{\eta}\mu a\tau os$ $a\dot{v}\tau o\hat{v}$) to read ولا قدروا

على خلاف قوله would seem to reflect the same kind of preoccupa-
tion to avoid any statement that would imply that the human agent
has, independently and of himself, any power to act apart from or
contrary to the will of God, in an almost classical, traditionalist
Muslim formulation.

A number of omissions are also noteworthy in that what has been
removed is precisely the mention of religious practice which is foreign
to Islam. Thus we find omitted 7.29b-31 where there is an exortation
to revere priests and faithfully to make certain offerings and sacrifices; 38.11, which also mentions sacrifices is likewise omitted as is
32.11b, where the tithe is mentioned. Following a somewhat similar
pattern, it is quite likely that 35.5-6 may have been dropped along
with 35.3b because of Islam's traditional disapproval of wine and
poetry. Again, although 24.8 is translated without alteration, it is
quite possible that 17.17bc, in which it is said that « He established
a leader for nation while the Lord's own portion is Israel » is dropped
because of the implication of the exclusive election of the Jews. Finally,
the paraphrasing translation of 28.15b, where for $\dot{e}\sigma\tau\acute{e}\rho\eta\sigma\epsilon\nu$ $a\dot{v}\tau\grave{a}s$ $\tau\hat{\omega}\nu$

---

[4] *Al-Fiqh al-Akbar*, § 6 (Hyderabad, 1373/1953, p. 3), translated in A. J. WENSINCK,
The Muslin Greed (Cambridge, 1932), 190 f.

[5] Cf. WENSINCK, *op. cit.*, 212 f; it is virtually impossible that the translation be
here in any way dependent upon the *Fiqh al-Akbar* since the present manuscript, allowing
the latest likely date (i.e., mid tenth century; cf. the preface to the text) would be nearly
contemporary with the latter (on whose date, cf. WENSINCK, *op. cit.*, 246 and L. GARDET
and G. ANAWATI, *Introduction à la théologie musulmane* [Paris, 1948], 141, n. 3) which,
therefore, would almost certainly have to be later than the original translation.

πονῶν αὐτῶν we find أَحْرِمِهِنَّ اولادهن واموالهن, is interesting because
of its explicit assumption that women hold private wealth; though
hardly fitting in a Jewish or Christian context of the period, this
is normal and, indeed, altogether appropriate in an Islamic context.

In the English translation I have attempted to maintain the general
tone of the Arabic version and consequently have preferred to follow,
insofar as is practical, the islamicising tendency of the Arabic text
rather to render it strictly as a translation by adhering always as
closely as possible to the literal sense of the Greek *Sirach*. Thus, for
example, I have, throughout, translated the term *mu'min* as « believer »
rather than, following the original εὐσεβής, as « godly, » « pious, » or
the like, *kâfir* as « unbeliever, » etc.; *sunna*, in all cases, I have left
untranslated, since there is no real English equivalent.[6] Because of the
interest that the version holds for the textual history of the Greek
Sirach, I have attempted to keep the English translation as literal
as possible, though certain inconsistencies are inevitable. One must
choose, even though, given the complexity of the text and its history,
any choice involves some loss and one might have valid reasons for
wishing the translation treated otherwise, whether in whole or in part.
It is hoped that it will prove adequate to the use of all who may have
occasion to consult it.

---

[6] The verb رفض, which occurs in various forms throughout the translation in place
of Greek βδέλυγμα forms a special problem; in some occurrences (e.g., 13.20) the use
is clear and the word is easily understood in its normal meaning but in others, where
the *maṣdar* is used (e.g., 15.13; 17.26) this is not the case; although one can under-
stand, in these places, the verbal noun *rafḍ* as a substantive, equivalent of the participle
marfûḍ, nevertheless, within the general context of the translation and its usage, it
evokes most readily the heresy of the *râfiḍa* (a term of usually pejorative character
that was applied to various šiʻite sects, to denote an intransigent refusal to follow the
common, orthodox Muslim doctrine concerning the first caliphs and, thereby, their
heresy in general). It is, indeed, difficult if not impossible to hear any other meaning for
the word in 15.13 where the expression *an-nifâq* is introduced along side *ar-rafḍ* and
where, as was noted above, the following verse is emended so as to give a thoroughly
Islamic formulation.

[The Wisdom of Ibn Sirach]

[... ...
(26) ...] for the Lord will nourish you with it. (27) Wisdom and instruction are the fear of the Lord; His good-pleasure is fidelity and meekness; (28) so do not contend against the fear of the Lord and do not
go to Him with a divided heart. (29) Do not be guileful and dissembling
in the mouths of men, but rather beware of your lips. (30) Do not extol
yourself lest you fall and draw disgrace and dishonor upon yourself
and the Lord reveal your secrets and disgrace you openly in the midst
of the community because you did not approach Him in fear but
rather your heart was filled with guile.

(1) My son, if you will draw near to the worship of God, prepare
in your soul for the trial. (2) Ready your heart, open it, and be patient.
Do not be anxious in the time of misfortune. (3) Rather, draw near
to Him, cleave to Him, and do not leave Him so that you may finally
grow great. (4) Whatever befalls you, receive it with joy and gladness;
then, be patient in the course of your humiliation, (5) for gold is
tested by fire and those that are found acceptable are tried in the
furnace of their humiliation. (6) Have faith in Him, for He will come
to your assistance. Make level your paths and put your trust in Him.

(7) O you who fear God, await His mercy and stray not away from
Him lest you fall. (8) O you who fear the Lord, have faith in Him, for
He will not reward you unjustly. (9) O you who fear the Lord, have
confidence * in the best and in eternal joy and the blessing of mercy. * f. 1 v°
(10) Then, behold the generations of old and consider whether
anyone ever put his trust in the Lord and was put to shame or anyone
was ever steadfast in the fear of Him and He then forsook him or
anyone ever called upon Him and He rejected him and paid him no
heed, (11) because the Lord is compassionate and merciful; He forgives
sins and brings salvation at the moment of distress and anxiety.

(12) Woe to the cowardly hearts and weak hands. Woe the sin which
goes in two divergent paths. (13) Woe the craven heart, for it does
not believe and therefore shall not be sheltered. (14) Woe to you, o
you who have done away with forebearance; what will you do when
the Lord visits you?

(15) Those who fear the Lord will never dispute His word and those

who love the *sunna* will keep His commandments. (16) Those who fear
the Lord will seek his good-pleasure and those who love Him will be
laden with the covenant of His *sunna*. (17) Those who fear the Lord
will prepare their hearts; they will humble themselves before Him
(18) saying « We shall fall into the hands of the Lord and not into the ₅
hands of men, for as is His majesty so also is His mercy ».

III   OF ONE'S FATHER AND MOTHER

(1) Listen attentively to your father, o children, and do thus so
that you may be saved. (2) The Lord has placed the father in honor
and dignity over his children and has confirmed the mother's judgment ₁₀
over her sons. (3) He, then, who honors his father, his sins shall be
* f. 2 rᵒ forgiven. * (4) He who reveres and honors his mother is like one
who lays up a treasure. (5) He who honors his father shall find joy in
his children and shall be answered on the day of his prayer. (6) He
who holds his father in honor shall live long and he who obeys God ₁₅
will give his mother repose (7) and will wait upon his parents as upon
his two masters.

(8) Honor your father in word and works so that from him a blessing
may come upon you, (9) for the blessing of a father makes firm the
households of his sons and a mother's curse uproots their foundations. ₂₀
(10) Take no pride in the shame of your parents for that is no honor
to you but rather shame. (11) A man will have honor from his honor-
ing his father and children's disgrace is from their contempt for their
mother. (12) My son, take care of your father in his old age and do not
grieve him during his lifetime. (13) If he be witless, excuse him and ₂₅
do not revile him with all your strength, as you are able, (14) for
mercy towards one's father will never be forgotten but will be an
edifice for you, built in the stead of your sins, (15) and he will remind
you of this in the moment of your distress. Like the bright sky over
the frost, so shall your sins be absolved. (16) He who neglects his ₃₀
father is like the blasphemer and a curse from God is upon him who
incites your mother to anger.

(17) O my son, accomplish your actions with meekness and humility
that you may be beloved by him who is acceptable. (18) In proportion
to your greatness humble yourself, for then you shall find the grace ₃₅

of mercy before God, (20) because the Lord * is great in power and
the humble glorify Him. (21) Do not seek what is too great for you;
do not search after what is too difficult for you. (22) Think rather on
what you have been commanded, for you have no need of those
₅ mysteries that are hidden from you. (23) Do not strive in matters that
are superfluous to your works, for understanding greater than that
of men will be made known to you. (24) How many are those whose
opinion has betrayed them and their thought brought down evil
opinion.

₁₀   (26) The hardened heart will turn evil in the end. Every one who
loves trouble will perish thereby. (27) The heardened heart is heavy
with miseries and the sinner adds sin to his sins. (28) There is no
healing for the disaster that strikes the proud man, since the root of
evil is grounded in him. (29) But the heart of the prudent man seeks
₁₅ understanding through parables while the desire of the wise man is
the attentive hearer. (30) Water quenches the blazing fire and alms
bring forgiveness of sins. (31) He who returns goodness will afterwards be remembered and will find shelter in the time of his downfall.

OF GIVING TO A POOR MAN   IV

₂₀   (1) My son, do not take from the pauper his livelihood and do not
turn your eyes from the needy beggar. (2) Do not grieve a naked,
hungry soul; do not anger a man who is destitute and poor. (3) Do not
anger an irascible heart. Do not refuse a gift to a beggar; (4) do not
send the beggar away when he is grieved nor turn your face * from
₂₅ the pauper. (5) Do not divert your eyes from the destitute pauper and
do not give any man occasion to curse you, (6) for if he curses you in
the anger of his soul his creator will answer his plea against you.

    (7) Then, make yourself loved by the community and lower your
head to the man of rank and power. (8) Make your ear attentive to the
₃₀ pauper and answer him justly with peace and meekness. (9) Rescue
the oppressed from the hands of the oppressor. Do not hold back in
seeking judgement. (10) But rather, be to orphans as their father and
to their widowed mother be like her husband and you shall become like
the son of the Most High and your mother will love you thereafter.

OF WISDOM

(11) Wisdom ennobles her sons and takes as her own those who long for her; (12) he who loves life and those who rise early to find her shall be filled with joy. (13) He who gets possession of her will inherit glory and the Lord will bless him wherever he goes. (14) The 5 Lord loves those who love her. (15) He who hears and obeys her will judge between the nations. He who is attentive to her shall find refuge in peace. (16) If he puts his trust in her, he shall inherit her and his people will be elevated in honor, (17) for at first she goes with him tortuously and raises up against him fear and fright and chastises him 10 with her instruction until his soul trusts in her; she tests him with her uprightness and her justice. (18) Then she returns to him with ease and straightness and makes him rejoice and she reveals her secrets and her mysteries to him. (19) If he wanders astray and casts off her restraint she will leave him and deliver him into the hands of his error 15 * f. 3 vᵒ * and his downfall.

OF SHAME AND THE GOOD USE OF TIME

(20) Use your time well and guard against evil. Do not be shamed on your own account, (21) for there is a shame that is an honor and a blessing. (22) Do not show favor to anyone to your own disadvantage. 20 Do not be put to shame at your own slip and downfall. (23) Do not refrain from speaking at the moment of salvation, (24) for wisdom is recognised only from speech and good training is manifested in what the tongue speaks. (25) Do not oppose the truth but be ashamed of your folly and ignorance. (26) Do not be ashamed to acknowledge 25 your own sins. Do not struggle against the force and vehemence of the river's rush. (27) Do not bare your soul to an ignorant, stupid man and do not show partiality to the man of rank and power. (28) Rather, strive for the sake of the truth, even to death, and God, the Lord, will fight to defend you at all times. (29) Do not be churlish, 30 overbearing, and over-insistent in your speech nor hapless and slack in your deeds. (30) Do not be like a lion in your house nor unreasonable, rude, or peevish with the people of your household.

(31) Neither let your hand be held out to take nor held tight closed
from giving. (1) Do not guard your wealth. Do not hoard it; do not   **V**
say « It is my complete sufficiency». (2) Do not give ready consent
to your inclinations or to your strength and do not follow after the
5 passion of your heart. (3) Do not say « Who is able to subdue me»,
for the Lord will take vengeance for your insolence. (4) Do not say
« I have sinned but what could befall me, for the Lord is long in
* patience». (5) Do not be unfearful of seeking forgiveness lest you * f. 4 rº
add sins to your sins. (6) Do not say therein that « His compassion is
10 great; He will pardon me and forgive me the multitude of my sins
and transgressions», for mercy and wrath are from Him and his anger
settles on sinners. (7) Do not delay turning to the Lord; do not put
this off from day to day, for the anger of the Lord goes forth suddenly
and while you delay it will strike you and crush you; you will perish
15 and pass away at the moment of vengeance. (8) Do not amass wealth
by injustice and oppression, for it will not benefit you at the time of
your misfortune.

(9) Do not winnow in every wind and do not follow every path.
Such, indeed, is the fork-tongued sinner. (10) Be serious in your com-
20 prehension and your understanding and let your word be one. (11) Be
quick to hear good and persistently give an honest reply. (12) If you
have understanding and comprehension, answer your companion
and if not, let your hand be over your mouth, (13) for honor and
dishonor are from talking and a man's tongue is his downfall and ruin.

25   OF THE SLANDERER

(14) Then, never in all your life be called a slanderer; do not lay
snares of deceit with your tongue, for disgrace falls upon the thief
while knowledge of evil belongs to the two-tongued. (15) Do not be   * f. 4 vº
unknowing of what is great * or trivial. (1) Do not become an enemy   **VI**
30 instead of a friend, for that will bequeath you a bad name, shame and
disgrace. Thus is the two-tongued sinner.

OF THE SOUL'S COUNSEL

(2) Then, do not exalt your soul in its counsel lest your soul be snatched away like a flash (3) and you then devour your foliage and destroy your fruit and your soul remain like a dried stick, (4) for an evil soul destroys its possessor and its enemies gloat over it, (5) but ₅ the gracious, gentle throat multiplies its friends and the articulate tongue increases goodly address.

OF INTIMATE COUNSEL AND FRIENDS

(6) Let those who are on amicable terms with you be many but those of your intimate counsel one in thousands. (7) If you acquire ₁₀ a friend, acquire him through a test and do not let your soul trust him too quickly, (8) for a man may be a friend in his own season but not stand fast by you in the moment of your distress. (9) A man may be a friend but then change and prove an enemy to you and reveal the unhappiness of your shame and thereby disgrace you (10) and a ₁₅ man may be a friend and companion at table but not stand fast by you in the moment of your distress. (11) Nay, he may be your very likeness when you are prosperous and gain dominance over the members of your private household (12) but if you humble yourself before him he will become your enemy; he will depart and be hidden from ₂₀ before you.

(13) Outstrip your enemies and beware of your friends, (14) for a trustworthy friend is a firm, strong shelter and he who finds him has ＊ f. 5 rᵒ found ＊ a treasure. (15) There is no measure of a trustworthy friend and no price nor can his goodness be weighed in the balance. (16) The ₂₅ trustworthy friend is a life-giving balm and those who fear the Lord shall find him. (17) He who fears the Lord is open in his friendship and his companion is like him, his intimate friend.

OF PROPER TRAINING AND WISDOM FROM YOUTH

(18) My son, choose yourself proper training from your youth and ₃₀ you shall surely find wisdom in your old age. (19) Draw near to her

like the ploughman, the sower, and await her pleasant fruits, for
little do you toil and labor at her work and quickly you will eat of her
yield. (20) Know that she is difficult and painful indeed to the ignorant nor can an unintelligent man stand firm before her. (21) Rather,
5 upon him she is like a stone of affliction, harshness and punishment,
and he does not delay to cast her quickly off from him. (22) Wisdom is
like her name and is not manifest to most or to the common crowd.

(23) Listen, my son, and accept my opinion; do not disdain my
counsel. (24) Place your foot in her fetters and your neck in her
10 collar. (25) Place your shoulders under her and carry her and her
harness will surely not be oppressive to you. (26) Nay, draw near to
her with all your heart and keep her ways with all your strength, (27)
for if you seek her out and make her yours she will become manifest
to you and when you have taken possession of her do not let her go,
15 (28) for ultimately then you will find her rest and her repose, because
she will turn to you with her kindness. * (29) Her fetters will become * f. 5 v°
for you a strong shelter and her harness a bright and glorious garment,
(30) because she is decked in gold and her fetters are thread spun with
gems. (31) You will clothe yourself with a robe of glory and you will
20 put on a crown of joy.

(32) You, my child, if you wish, will become learned and, if you
discipline your soul to work, you will become clever and shrewd. (33)
If you take pleasure in listening you will wait for understanding and
if your ear is attentive you will become wise. (34) If you are present
25 in a company of mature men attend fully to the wisest of them. (35)
You will delight in listening to every godly tale and wise parables
will not escape you. (36) If you see an intelligent man, rise before
dawn to go to him and let your feet be directed frequently to the
stairs of his portals. (37) In sacred matters be learned in the highest
30 degree and speak of His commandments at all times; He will strenthen
your heart and make it steadfast and your longing for wisdom will be
fulfilled. (1) Do no evil and evil will not befall you. (2) Yea, turn   **VII**
away from the wicked, unjust man and he will depart from you.

OF WICKEDNESS AND INJUSTICE

35 (3) My son, sow not in the furrows of injustice and wickedness and
you shall not reap sevenfold of them. (4) Seek not from the Lord a

position of high authority nor seek from a king a place of honor. (5) Do
not hold yourself just before the Lord and do not pretend wisdom
before a king. (6) Do not seek to become a judge lest perchance you
prove incapable of doing away with injustice or perchance you be
* f. 6 rᵒ overawed * at the presence of the powerful man of rank and so act 5
shamefully and cast doubt on your own integrity. (7) Sin not and do
no evil among a city's people and do not disparage yourself publicly.

(8) Do not be content with asking twice for absolution of your sins
for you shall never be held just thereby. (9) Do not say « He will regard
the multitude of my gifts; when I approach God, the Most High, 10
He will receive me and forgive me ». (10) Do not be hesitant when
you pray; do not put off your almsgiving. (11) Do not mock an irascible man, for God is the one who exalts and He is the one who humbles.

OF LYING

(12) Do not deceive your brother with lies and do not do any such 15
thing to your friend. (13) Do not desire to tell one single lie, for no good
comes of such a habit. (14) Be not overanxious in the company of
older men and do not proliferate words when you pray. (15) Do not
loathe a task which is arduous and demanding nor cultivating the
soil, which the Most High has made. (16) Do not count yourself in 20
the society of the sinful, but rather remember that wrath will surely
not long be held back from the unbelievers. (17) Humble yourself and
be humble indeed, for the vengeance on the unbelievers and the sinful
is fire and maggot. (18) Do not seek another friend in exchange for a
devoted friend of yours nor for one of your brethren fine pure gold.   25

OF WIFE AND SLAVE AND HIRED MAN

(19) Then, do not fail to get a good, wise wife, for her favor is better
and of more worth than gold. (20) Do not mistreat your faithful slave
* f. 6 vᵒ * who works as he ought nor a hired man who applies himself assidu-
ously. (21) On the contrary, your soul should love the intelligent 30
slave; do not deny him nor deprive him of manumission.

(22) Then, if you possess riding animals, see to their needs and if you have need of them, keep them. (23) If you have sons, train them and bend their necks from their childhood. (24) If you have daughters, keep watch over their bodies and do not show them a laughing, smiling
5 face. (25) Give your daughter in marriage; you will have accomplished a great task. But see that you give her to a prudent and understanding husband. (26) If you have a wife who suits your soul's desire do not put her away from you, but in no matter of yours trust a woman who despises you.
10 (27) Then, revere your father and honor him with all your heart and do not forget your mother's pangs of labor. (28) Nay, remember that you were born of her. How can you in return do for her as she has done for you ?

OF THE FEAR OF GOD AND GOOD WORKS

15 (29) Then, fear God with all your soul. (32) Extend your hand to the pauper in order that your blessing may be perfect. (33) Let the generosity of your gifts be before every living man. Do not withhold your generosity from the dead. (34) Do not hold yourself back from those who weep, but rather mourn with those who mourn. (35) Do
20 not refrain from visiting the sick, because for such conduct you will be
* loved. (36) Remember your end in all your discourse and do not * f. 7 r⁰
ever sin.

OF THE ARROGANT
AND THE WEALTHY AND THE STUPID   VIII

25 (1) Do not contend with a powerful, arrogant man and do not fall into his hands. (2) Do not enter into a dispute with a wealthy man, lest poverty and need become your companions through the paucity of your possessions, for gold has destroyed and ruined many men and has led astray the hearts of kings. (3) Do not joke with a glib, dissolute
30 man nor heap wood on his kindled fire. (4) Do not joke with a stupid, foolish man, lest your fathers and forefathers be dishonored.

OF TURNING TO REPENTANCE

(5) Do not revile a man who turns from sin to repentance, but rather remember that all of us are sinners and bound to judgement. (6) Show no contempt for a man in his old age, for old men shall come from among us. (7) Do not gloat at a man's death, but rather remember 5 that all of us shall die. (8) Do not spurn the tales of wise men and their sayings, but rather review their parables and consider their import, for from them you shall learn good training and instruction and so may with ease become the servant of men of power and high rank. (9) Do not find fault with the talk of old men, for they have learned 10 from their fathers and from them you shall learn wisdom and understanding.

OF GIVING A REPLY

Then, give a reply when it is due. (10) Do not enkindle the coals of the sinful man lest you be burned by the flame of his fire. (11) Do not 15 depart from the presence of a man who reviles you lest the fire of his

* f. 7 v° opposition * take rule of your mouth.

(12) Lend no money to a man stronger than yourself, but if you do, count it as something lost to you. (13) Do not make a pledge beyond your capacity, but if you do, prepare yourself as does the one who 20 will fulfill his pledge. (14) Do not contend with a judge or enter into litigation with him, for they will render judgement in his favor according to his rank.

(15) Do not travel with a reckless man, lest his evil weigh heavy upon you because of his wrongdoing, for he will act only by his wish 25 and whim and you will perish on account of his foolishness and recklessness. (16) Do not contend with a hot-headed, violent-tempered man; do not go out with him into the desert, for blood is as nothing in his eyes and there he will strike you down where there is no one to aid you. 30

(17) Do not take counsel with a stupid man, for he will not be capable of patience and of bearing with your discourse. (18) Do not reveal your secret before a stranger, for you do not know what will come of

it in the future. (19) Do not reveal to every one what is in your heart and may no one seek your favor with lying.

(1) Then, do not be jealous of the wife of your embrace lest you **IX** teach her bad habits to your own disadvantage. (2) Do not give a
5 woman mastery over yourself, lest she come to despise your force and your strength. (3) Avoid a libidinous, immoral woman lest you fall into her snares. (4) Do not be alone with a woman who is prone to make accusations, lest you be seduced by her wiles and she lead you into temptation. * (5) Do not enquire after a nubile young woman * f. 8 rᵒ
10 lest you fall under suspicion and doubt from her censure. (6) Do not put yourself into the hands of harlots lest you destroy your inheritance from your parents. (7) Do not cast your glance down the backstreets of the city lest you wander astray and go to excess in its waste. (8) Avert the glance of your eye from the loveliness and beauty of a woman
15 and do not gaze intently after beauty that is not yours. [...]

(1) [...] and the rule of the intelligent man is lastening and stable. **X**
(2) As is the judge of the people, so are his ministers and as is the governor of the city, so are its inhabitants. (3) The king who is without education destroys his people and cities prosper through the widom
20 and understanding of their leaders. (4) The dominion of the Earth is in the hand of the Lord to raise up and make ruler over it the able and competent in his turn. (5) Man's well-being and guidance are in the hand of the Lord and the faces of learned secretaries get them honor.

OF INJUSTICE AND PRIDE

25 (6) Harbor no rancor against your neighbor because of any word or unjust act; and do not do anything at all to revile and offend, (7) for pride is hateful to God and men and wrongdoing and oppression, injustice and enmity arise from it. (8) Dominion passes from one people to another because of oppression, offence, and wealth. (9) Why should
30 earth and ashes hold themselves in high esteem, * he who in his life abhors what was hidden in his own belly?

(10) The physician scoffs at a sickness when it is long drawn out. To day the king and tomorrow he will die (11) and a man, when he dies, falls heir to reptiles, maggots, and dust. (12) The beginning
35 of a man's pride is his separation from his Lord and his heart's separ-

ation from his Creator. (13) The beginning of sin is pride and he who perseveres in it lays up a hoard of disgrace. Therefore the Lord has glorified the misfortunes of the proud and has destroyed them utterly. (14) He has cast down the *minbars* of the mighty, those who are proud, and made the humble sit upon them in their stead. (15) He has made barren the roots of arrogant nations and raised up in their place the humble. (16) He has devastated the land of haughty nations and has uprooted them and annihilated them to the foundations of the earth (17) and has withdrawn them from them, annihilated and destroyed them, and has expunged their memory from the earth, (18) for pride was not created for mankind nor the rage of anger and wrath for the sons of women.

OF PROGENY

(19) The righteous progeny is the progeny of mankind and the firm-founded progeny is the progeny of those who fear the Lord. To those who love Him belong the gracious shoots. The despicable progeny belongs to those who do not keep the *sunna*. The goodly, righteous progeny belongs to the God-fearing and the contemptible progeny * belongs to those who transgress the commandments. (20) The eyes of the Lord are upon those who fear Him. (22) The boast of the foreigner, the poor man, and the noble is the fear of the Lord.

* f. 9 rᵒ

OF THE POOR, THE MAN OF RANK, AND THE SLAVE

(23) It is not just to despise a poor man who is wise nor is it proper to honor a sinful man, (24) for the high official, the judge, and the man of rank shall be honored but the best of them and the greatest is the one who fears the Lord. (25) Free men serve the intelligent slave. The man of understanding does not murmur or grumble nor does he become angry.

OF GAINING WEALTH

(26) Then, do not make pretence of wisdom for doing your work and do not put on an air of superiority in your time of distress, (27) for he who labors and earns and has an abundance of worldly goods is better than another; he is more honorable than the one who makes a show of superiority while asking for bread. (28) With humility hold your soul in honor and esteem it, my son; give it respect as is fitting. (29) Who considers him blameless who wrongs himself or who shows respect for him who despises his own life? (30) The pauper is honored for his wisdom; the rich man is honored for his wealth. (31) If, then, an indigent man is respected in his indigence, how much more will a rich man be respected in his wealth and if a rich man is not respected in his wealth, how much more will the indigent not be respected in his indigence? (1) A poor man's wisdom will raise him up and will seat **XI** him in the midst of the mighty.

OF WHAT IS PRAISEWORTHY AND CONTEMPTIBLE

(2) Then, do not praise * a man for his comeliness and do not * f. 9 v⁰ despise a man on account of his appearance. (3) The smallest of all flying creatures is the bee but her fruit is the foremost of sweets. (4) Do not boast of the apparel you wear and do not exalt yourself because of any dignity of rank, for the deeds of the Lord are wonderous and lie hidden among the sons of mankind. (5) Many have sat on the earth ¹ and those whose position had been unknown have been clothed with the diadem; (6) many of the mighty have been severely humilated and the nobles have been delivered into the hands of others.

(7) Make no blame or reproach before you enquire and make certain; ascertain first, rather, then blame and rebuke. (8) Make no reply before hearing. Do not be forward in the midst of a discourse (9) and do not dispute concerning a matter which causes you no grief. Do not sit in council with the wicked during their litigation. (10) My son, let

---

¹ Sic; τύραννοι >.

not your actions and efforts be in diversified things, for if you multiply
them you will not be blameless and if you seek them you will never
get them.

OF ONE WHO LABORS AND TOILS

(11) There is, among men, one who labors and toils and is industrious ₅
but who, all the while, is indigent and penniless. (12) There is also,
among men, one who is dull, indolent and needs assistance. There is
among men one who is destitute of power, weak, and of great poverty
indeed; the eyes of the Lord look favorably upon him to raise him up
* f. 10 r⁰ and rescue him from this poverty of his (13) and He will lift up * his ₁₀
head from distress and many men will be astonished when they see
him, (14) for life and death, poverty and wealth are from the Lord;
(15) from Him is wisdom too and understanding and the knowledge
of the *sunna* and from Him is love and the way of righteous actions.
(16) Those, however, who exalt themselves in doing evil, evil shall ₁₅
abide with them. (17) The Lord's gift remains fast with those who
worship Him with true devotion; His good-pleasure will assist them
forever.

OF WEALTH

(18) There is among men the one who has become wealthy through ₂₀
his fortitude and the greatness of his avarice; it is his lot and from it
is his reward, (19) in that he has said « I have found repose and now
I will eat of my goods » without knowing what moment will carry
him off to die and leave it to someone else. (20) So hold fast to
your charge and tell it abroad and grow old in your labor. (21) Do not ₂₅
admire the works of the sinful but rather trust in the Lord and be
steadfast in your endeavor, for it is easy and light for the Lord to
enrich the pauper. (22) The blessing of the Lord is in the wages of
the believers and in a quick, fleeting moment He will show forth His
blessing. (23) Do not say within your heart « Of whom might I have ₃₀
need ? » or « What wordly goods will now come to be mine ? » (24) and

do not say either « What I have is sufficient for me; why should I
torment myself henceforth ? », (25) since evil is not perceived on the
day of good fortune nor is good fortune perceived on the day of evil,
(26) for it is easy for God to requite * a man on the day of his   * f. 10 vº
5 death according to his ways. (27) The death of a man will reveal his
action. (28) Do not, then, say to a man before his death « Blessed are
you ». The criterion for knowing a man is his children.

(29) Do not bring every man into your house, for the snares and
traps of Iblîs are many. (30) Like the partidge which one hunts
10 with a basket, thus does he watch the heart of the proud and like a spy,
thus he will observe his downfall. (31) He will turn good to evil with
his watching and produce deceit in him in whom there is none. (32)
Lime is produced in abundance from the ashes of fire and the watching
of the sinful man is blood. (33) Beware therefore of the wicked man
15 who works evil, lest he bring shame and eternal disgrace upon you,
for he plots an evil scheme (34) and of the man who dwells with
you and of the man who accompanies you, when he is a stranger, lest he
change your state to unrest and misfortune and alienate you from your
own house and your intimates.

20   OF ACTS OF GOODNESS   XII

(1) Then, if you do good, consider him to whom you do it, so that
there may be bounty in your wordly goods. (2) Do good to the indigent
believer and you shall find recompense; if he does not reward you,
the Most High will reward you. (3) Indeed, he who carefully plots
25 an evil scheme shall have no prosperity. Make, then, no gift and bestow
no alms on him who has no mercy, * (4) but rather give to the indigent   * f. 11 rº
believer; do not aid the sinner. (5) Do good to the pauper and do not
give to the unbeliever, but rather withold his loaves of bread and
do not give them to him, lest he dominate you and overpower you
30 thereby; for you will find you have evil, secretly, in double measure
for all the good you have done him. (6) The Most High hates the
sinful and will requite the unbelievers with vengeance.

OF FRIEND AND ENEMY

(8) Then, a friend is not recognized in time of prosperity and an enemy is not concealed in time of misfortune. (9) When a man is in distress his friends will leave him and when he is in prosperity his enemies are grieved. (10) So, never feel safe from your enemy, for 5 his evil is like the poison of brass. (11) Do not feel safe from him if he humbles himself before you and walks with lowered head. Beware of him, then, and be on watch against him; be to him a fighting opponent, looking at him as you look at a mirror; then you will realise that he has finally rusted. (12) Do not bring him near you and do 10 not give him a place opposite you, lest he drive you away and sit in your place, nor give him a seat at your right hand, lest he seek your seat; for ultimately you shall know my discourse and shall wonder at my word and repent.

(13) Who pities the snake-charmer who allows himself to be bitten 15 * f. 11 v⁰ by a snake or anyone who * approaches a wild beast? (14) So also no one pities him who walks in the company of a sinful man or him who sullies himself with his sins, (15) because he will, indeed, stand fast with you in time of righteousness and justice, but if you absent yourself from him he will not restrain himself from injustice. (16) An 20 enemy talks sweetly with his lips while he plots in his heart how he will dig you a pit in which to bury you, all the while weeping and his eyes pouring tears, but if he finds his moment or opportunity he will never be sated with blood. (17) If misfortune should befall you he will be there ahead of you as if to give help, as he digs you a 25 hole under your very heels; (18) he will shake his head and clap his hands and calculate many things, as his expression changes.

XIII   OF THE PROUD AND THE WEALTHY MAN

(1) He who touches pitch defiles himself and he who associates with the proud man becomes like him. (2) So, do not carry a weight 30 that you do not find light and do not associate with a man who is stronger than you and more wealthy than you. How shall an earthen-ware pot associate with a brass pot, since the one will knock and the

other break ? (3) The rich man is the oppressor, as he becomes abusive, and the pauper is the oppressed, as he asks and begs. (4) If you are well off, the rich man will do business with you but if hardship or poverty befalls you, he will leave you (5) and take away what you
5 possess without suffering anything himself and without being grieved in any way on your account. * (6) If he needs you he will seduce you * f. 12 rᵒ and mislead you; he will mock you and inspire you with hope; he will speak kind words to you and say to you « What is your need ? » (7) and you will be shamed and disgraced from the great variety of his
10 food until, two or three times, he takes away what you possess. Finally he will satirize you and afterwards he will look at you and leave you. Then he will shake his head over you. (8) So beware of being over-weening and erring in your opinion and thought, but do not humble yourself before him either in the joy of your heart.

15   OF THE PERSON OF RANK

(9) When a person of rank summons you, excuse yourself and do not show him that you want him, for he will long for you all the more and will call you to himself. (10) Beware lest you slip and fall in his presence and he cast you off; but do not remain at a distance from him
20 lest he forget you. (11) Do not fail to greet him but do not be believ-ing of the greater part of what he says, for he will test you with much talking order to draw out your opinion, will try to discover your inmost thoughts, as if facetiously, (12) and will retain what you say, getting it by guile. (13) Beware of him and be very much on your guard in
25 his respect, (15) for every animal loves only its like and every man loves only his kinsman and his fellow.
(16) Every corporeal creature joins only with one of like kind and a man cleaves only to his like. (17) How, then, shall the wolf be associate of the lamb ? How shall the sinner be associate of the believer
30 * (18) and how shall the rich man be at peace with the poor ? (19) * f. 12 vᵒ The prey of lions is the wild asses in the desert and the prey of the rich is the poor. (20) As the proud reject the pauper, so do the wealthy reject the poor. (21) When the rich man weakens his intimates streng-then him; (22) when he sins by a word those who would help him
35 are many and when he utters monstrous things they justify him. But

as for the poor man, when he has neither sinned nor done evil they berate him and when he speaks out the truth and wisdom they make no place for him and do not allow him to speak. (23) When the rich man speaks they all keep silent and extol his discourse to the clouds. When the pauper speaks they say « Who is this ? » and when he slips 5 they mistreat him. (24) Wealth is just whenever there is no sin in it. How harsh is penury and want for the believing freeman; how loathsome is poverty in the mouths of the unbelievers.

(25) A man's heart alters his face, be it by reason of goodness or be it by reason of evil. (26) The traces of goodness and righteousness 10 are in the heart when the face is smiling and radiant. Wise parables and their understanding come about only through weariness and toil.

XIV (1) Blessed is a man who has not been pained by the sadness of sin.

(2) Blessed is he whose soul has not rebuked him and he who has not [* f. 13 r⁰ fallen from his hope and his trust in his Lord. *   15

OF THE GRUDGING MISERLY MAN

(3) Wealth ill becomes a man of trivial speech. For what does a grudging, miserly man have riches? (4) He who amasses from himself merely amasses for others; others will live luxuriously on his worldly goods. (5) He who treats himself badly, whom will he treat 20 well? He will not rejoice in his worldly goods. (6) There is no one more wicked than him who is miserly towards himself and this is the reward of his evil and wickedness. (7) If he does some good thing it is merely a lapse on his part; afterwards, he will finally manifest his evil and wickedness. (8) The grudging, avaricious man is the wicked man; 25 he turns his face away from souls and rejects them.

OF THE EXCESSIVELY GREEDY MAN

(9) The eye of the excessively greedy man cannot be satisfied but rather his wrongdoing, injustice, and wickedness wither his soul and dry him up. (10) The wicked eye is envious of food but its spread table 30 is wanting, lacking of it.

(11) So, my son, do what is best, according to your means, and
offer sacrifice to God as is required. (12) Remember that death will
not tarry and that the promise of hell-fire will be manifested to you;
(13) so, do good to your friend before your death; extend your hand
5 and give to him according to your ability. (14) Do not hold back
from a joyous day and let no portion of wholesome desire escape you.
(15) Shall you not leave your toil and labor to another and your gain
and your labor for the division of lots? (16) So give and take and
sanctify your soul, * for the pleasure of life is not to be sought in * f. 13 vᵒ
10 hell-fire. (17) The end of each body is that it be worn out like a garment and the covenant from the beginning of time is "surely you
shall die". (18) Like the leaves of the trees in a luxuriant wood — one
falls away and another grows in its place — thus is the race of flesh
and blood; one is born and another dies. (19) The term of every
15 work is towards decay and death and with it he who did it dies and
passes away.

OF THE BLESSEDNESS THAT BELONGS TO WISDOM

(20) Blessed is the man who dies in his wisdom and the one who
speaks his every utturance in wisdom and understanding with holiness.
20 (21) Blessed is he who considers her ways in his heart and he whose
thought considers her secrets, (22) and he who goes forth on her
tracks like a man on a quest and he who keeps watch on her ways,
(23) for he who looks out from her windows and listens at her portals
(24) and settles in the proximity of her house and fastens pegs in her
25 walls, (25) it is he who will erect his tent in her hands and will settle
in a wholesome dwelling; (26) he will raise sons in her shelter; he
will be established under her branches and boughs. (27) Under her
canopy he will be sheltered from the heat and he will dwell in her
grace. (1) He who fears the Lord will do all this. He who acquires   **XV**
30 knowledge shall find her (2) and she will go out to meet him like
his mother. She will receive him * like a virgin woman (3) and will * f. 14 rᵒ
feed him the bread of understanding and give him the water of wisdom
to drink. (4) He will rely upon her and will not waver and will follow
her lead and will not be put to shame; (5) she will raise him up
35 and give him honor well above his fellows and she will open his mouth

in the midst of the mighty (6) with joy and the crown of gladness
and will bestow upon him an everlasting name. (7) Foolish men do
not perceive her, sinful men do not gaze upon her, (8) and lying men
do not remember her.

(9) Praise is unseemly in the mouths of sinners since it is not sent 5
from the Lord (10) and because praise is spoken only through wisdom;
through the Lord alone is it saved from unbelief. (11) Do not say,
therefore, « My unbelief is because of the Lord alone » for you do not
desire to effect what you hate and find distasteful. (12) Do not say
« He it is who led me astray and seduced me », for He has no need of 10
a sinful man. (13) The Lord hates all hypocrisy and sectarian
heresy nor do those who fear Him love this. (14) He it is who
created man in the beginning; then He commanded him and forbade
him. (15) So, if you wish, you will keep the commandments and will
keep trust and the faith of good-pleasure, (16) because He has set 15
before you fire and water and you will extend your hand where you
wish. (17) Life and death lie before man and whichever of them
* f. 14 vo delights him shall be given him. * (18) The wisdom of the Lord is
abundant and He is the Mighty, the Powerful in His might. He watches
everything. (19) His eyes are upon those who fear Him and He it is 20
who knows every act of man. (20) He has commanded no one any
unbelief in order that he should be unbelieving in Him nor has He
granted to any one license to commit sin.

XVI   OF SINFUL MEN

(1) And so, my son, do not long after the multitude of sinners and 25
do not take joy in the sons of the unbelievers (2) if they are numerous,
but only if the fear of the Lord comes to be in them. (3) Have no
confidence in their life and do not be pleased at their multitude, for
one righteous man is better than thousands of sinners. That you die
without having children is better for you than that you have children 30
who are unbelievers, (4) for through one wise man a city may thrive
but the tribe of the hypocrites will be desolate. (5) My eye has beheld
many things like these and my ear has heard stronger than them. (6)
Fire is enkindled in the community of the sinful and wrath blazes
up in the contentious nation.   35

(7) The Lord had no pity on the great warriors of old who dis-
believed in Him because of their might (8) nor had He pity on
the country of Lot and his place of refuge. These are those whom He
rejected because of their pride. (9) He did not have mercy on the
5 nation of the doomed, who were vanquished in their sins; * (10) * f. 15 rº
He destroyed six hundred thousand foot-soldiers, those who had all
come to be of one mind in the hardness of their hearts. (11) Strange,
then, would it be if you are found just while you are hard of heart.
Mercy and anger are from Him; He has power to forgive sins and
10 hold back anger. (12) As is the quantity of His mercy, so also is
the quantity of His reproof. He judges man according to his works.
(13) The sinner does not escape from Him with his theft and the
patient hope of the believers is not put off. (14) Rather, He makes a
place for each act of mercy and each man shall receive in accordance
15 with his works. (17) Do not then say « I shall hide from my Lord »
and « Who is it who will remember me from on high ? » and « Within the
multitude of the nation I shall not be recognised » and « What might
my soul be among innumerable creatures ? », (18) for heaven and the
heaven of heaven and the earth and the depths tremble at His scrutiny,
20 (19) together with the mountains and the foundations of the earth.
When He looks at them they quake with trembling. (20) The heart
meditates on this, saying « Who is it who will ponder His ways
(21) and who is it who will behold His whirlwinds, since the multitude
of His works is hidden and concealed ? (22) Who is it who will tell of
25 piety and justice or who is steadfast in His covenant, for it is far removed
from us ? » (23) But the imperfect heart does not ponder these things.
* The foolish, erring man ponders foolishness.   * f. 15 vº

OF THE JUDGEMENT AND WORKS OF THE LORD

(24) Listen to me, my son, and learn wisdom and with your heart be
30 attentive to my words, (25) for I shall show you proper training with
the scales and tell you with the certitude of wisdom and understanding
(26) that the Lord's judgement of His works is from the very first.
From the moment He created them he set aside their portions. (27)
He adorned His works for ever. He made their beginning in their
35 eras and His creatures neither hungered nor labored. They did not

leave off their works; (28) neither did any one of them grieve his
fellow nor were they capable of doing contrary to His word forever.
(29) Thereafter the Lord surveyed the earth and filled it with His
good things. (30) He covered its face with the souls of all animals and

XVII to it He made their returning. (1) The Lord's creation of man was 5
from the earth and then He returned him to it again. (2) He gave
His creatures a period of days and seasons and gave them rule over
whatever is in it. (3) He clothed them especially in strength and
created them in His own likeness. (4) He put the fear of Himself in
every mortal and gave them dominion over the wild beasts and the 10
birds. (6) He gave them discernment and language, eyes and ears
and understanding, so that they might reflect and comprehend. (7)
Then, indeed, He filled them with comprehension and understanding
and showed them good and evil. (8) He set His eyes upon their hearts
in order to show them the glories of His works. (11) He gave them 15
increase of comprehension and understanding and made them heir
to the *sunna* of life. (12) For them he made fast His promise for ever

* f. 16 rᵒ and He showed them His judgement. * (13) Their eyes beheld the
most magnificent glory and their ears heard His blessed voice.
(14) He commanded them and said, « Beware of all injustice », and He 20
enjoined them concerning one another. (15) Their ways are before
Him at every moment and they are not concealed from before His
eyes, (19) because His eyes are constantly upon their ways. (20)
Their injustice is not hidden from Him; all of their sins are before the
Lord. (22) To Him man's act of mercy is like a seal; like the apple 25
of His eye He cherishes his generosity. (23) Hereafter, He will raise
them up and give them their due and will requite them their due
upon their heads. (24) He has fixed a way for the penitent and He
has consoled those who forebearingly despair. (25) So turn to the
Lord and abandon sin; humble yourself before Him; seek His face 30
and diminish error. (26) Approach the Most High; withdraw from
injustice and despise sectarian heresy.

OF HELL-FIRE AND DEATH

(27) Who will glorify the Most High in hell-fire in place of the
living who give thanks, (28) since gratitude and desire vanish from 35

a dead man as if he had never been at all? So praise the Lord while
you are still alive and well, (29) for the mercy of the Lord is immense
and He is forgiving to those who return to Him; (30) all things
are not found in the son of man since the son of man is not immortal so
5 as not to die.

(31) What is more brilliant than the sun? but even it shall perish. Thus
will he perish who ponders on flesh and blood. (32) It is by the power
of the Lord that the rising of heaven returns. * All mankind is dust * f. 16 v°
and decay. (1) He who is the One who lives forever; He created **XVIII**
10 everything whatsoever; (2) He alone is the Lord, the Pious, the
Righteous, the Just. (4) No one has He made able to recount His
works or to search out His mighty deeds. (5) Who is it who will
reckon the power of His majesty or who will go further to recount
His mercy? (6) There is no one who can add or detract and no one
15 who can search out the marvels of the Lord.

OF HUMAN OPINION AND LIFE

(7) Whenever, in his opinion, he is done, then man begins; whenever he stops and rests, then what he seeks escapes him so that
he cannot attain it. (8) What, then, is man? What is his end? What
20 is his good and what his evil? (9) The number of man's days and
the multitude of his years is a hundred years. (10) That is
like a drop of water from the sea, like a grain of sand; such are a
few years in the days of eternity. (11) Therefore God has extended his
forebearance with his creatures and has poured out His mercy upon
25 them. (12) He has known and recognized that their changing is
wicked and therefore He has multiplied His forgiveness. (13) Man's
mercy is only towards a man like himself but God's mercy is upon
every mortal; it is He who rebukes and disciplines and teaches and
returns like the shepherd to his flock. (14) He has mercy upon those
30 who await instruction and upon those who hasten to His judgements.

OF GIVING

(15) My son, put no * defect in goodness and do not make a doleful * f. 17 r°
speech with every gift you give, (16) for just as the dew gives rest

from the heat, so does the statement excell the gift. (17) The good
statement excells the gift and the good statement excells the righteous
gift; both of them belong to the prosperous man, (18) but the fool
finds fault with no praise and the envious man's gift blinds his eyes.
(19) So, make certain and know well before you speak. Take care of 5
yourself and seek remedies before you become ill. (20) Test yourself
before the judgement, for you will find forgiveness in your hour of
distress. (21) Humble yourself before you become ill and show repentance in the time of sins. (22) Do not refrain from completing your
prayer at its proper time and do not remain unjustified until death. 10
(23) Prepare yourself before you pray; do not be like a man who
would put his Lord to the test. (24) Rather, remember your Lord's
wrath before your death and remember vengeance when His face
is turned away from you. (25) Remember the time of hunger in the
time of plenty and remember poverty and need in days of prosperity, 15
(26) for time changes from dawn to evening and every thing hurriedly
hastens before God. (27) The wise man fears His Lord in all circum-
stances and restrains himself from transgressions in days of sins.
* f. 17 vº (28) Every * intelligent man has come to recognise wisdom and
whenever he finds her he gives thanks. (29) The learned have shown 20
themselves wise through their discourse and they have multiplied
for themselves parables with their certainty.

OF PASSION

(30) Do not go in the track of your passions but rather restrain
yourself from your pleasures, (31) for if you give your soul over to 25
the good-pleasure of its passion you will cause your enemies to gloat
over you. (32) So do not rejoice or be delighted in abundance of luxury
XIX lest it make you, as it were, a prisoner through concern for it. (33) Do
not become indigent because of debts of money that you borrow,
lest you have nothing for your sufficiency, (1) for the drunken work- 30
man will never become wealthy and he who despises the little will
quickly fall. (2) Wine and women seduce intelligent men. There is
none more headstrong than the one who persues harlots; (3) he shall
inherit maggots and decay. The headstrong soul shall be destroyed and
shall perish.   35

OF THE FRIVOLOUS MAN

(4) He who assents quickly to a statement is light-headed, frivolous; he who sins and transgresses harms only himself. (5) The one to be censured is he who delights in what is wicked. (6) He who abhors evil
5 discourse will do little evil. (7) So never utter an evil word twice and you shall never be wanting. (8) Speak neither to your friend about your enemy nor to your enemy about your friend. If you have no sin, do not disclose it (9) lest the one who listens hear you * and come to * f. 18 r⁰ dispise you from that hour. (10) When you hear a word consider it
10 dead; be at ease and stand fast, for it will not make you burst.

OF THE FOOL

(11) The fool, when he hears a word, is seized with pangs just as a woman has pangs when she gives birth. (12) As an arrow is lodged in the body's thigh, so will a word be in the heart of a fool; he will be
15 incapable of bearing it.

OF ADMONISHING A FRIEND

(13) Do not admonish your friend; perhaps he did not do as you heard, and if he did do so, he will not again. (14) Admonish your companion; perhaps he did not speak as you heard, and if he did, he
20 will not do so again. (15) Admonish your friend, for frequently it has been slander. Do not believe every word, (16) for a man may blunder without its being his fault. Who is there who has not erred with his tongue ?

(20) The whole of wisdom is the fear of the Lord; He it is who makes
25 the *sunna* in all wisdom. (22) There is no wisdom that teaches evil nor is there understanding and intelligence in the deliberation of sinners. (23b) The stupid man is he who is lacking in wisdom. (24) The intelligent, god-fearing man is better and more virtuous than the one who has great knowledge but acts contrary to the *sunna*.

OF WRONGDOING

(23a) There is that wrongdoing that is outcast (25) and there is
that wrongdoing that is openly shameless, being unjust and oppressive,
* f. 18 v⁰ * like him who will pervert a favor in order that the judgement may
be made evident. (26) He will walk with evil, his head lowered, ₅
brooding darkly, his belly full of deceit (27) and his countenance
saddened, silent and hushed so as to overtake you and come upon you,
you know not where. (28) If he is prevented from something for lack
of strength, he will refrain and if he finds an opportunity he will do you
harm.   ₁₀

OF KNOWING A MAN

(29) A man is known from his appearance; the prudent, understanding man is known from encountering his face. (30) A man is
known from his attire and the laughter of his teeth; the manner of
XX   his walk will give you notice of him. (1) A man may be silent though ₁₅
wise and prudent.   (3) He who avows his religion is restrained from
evil. (4) As the desire of a eunuch is to deflower a virgin with his
garments, thus is he who renders his judgement by force. (5) A man
who remains silent you may find wise and another may be hated for his
talking too much. (6) Another may remain silent for lack of a reply ₂₀
and another may remain silent, being aware of the moment. (7a) The
wise man is silent up to the proper moment. (8a) He who talks a
great deal is scorned. (13a) The wise man is loved for his discourse
(7b) but the witless fool acts out of season.

OF A FOOL'S CHARITY   ₂₅

* f. 19 r⁰   (13b) The charities of a fool are handed over like merchandise. *
(14) The gift of a fool is not beneficial since his eyes show the one as
many. (15) He gives little and criticizes much; he opens his mouth
like a crying herald; he lends today and demands payment tomorrow.
The man who is like this is hated.   ₃₀

OF THE IGNORANT FOOL

(16) The ignorant fool says, « I have no friend nor have my goods any favor; those who eat my food are wanton of tongue ». (17) How many times his guests have laughed at him. (19) He is ever in the
5 mouths of the ignorant. (20) A parable is vile and base from the mouth of a fool; he does not tell it in its time or season. (21) There may be a man who is restrained from sin because of his poverty; he does not recall his end nor reflect on it. (22) There may be a man who destroys his soul through shame and destroys it on account of a stupid man. (23)
10 There is among men the one who becomes a friend on account of shame and the fool takes him as an enemy for nothing.

OF LYING

(24) Among men, lying is a wicked vice; it is forever found in the mouths of ignorant fools. (25) A thief is more virtuous than a man
15 who is habituated to constant lying; perdition will be the heir of both of them. (26) When a man is a liar, his mien is foul; * his shame * f. 19 v° abides with him forever. (27) The wise man is far superior to him in his speech. The wise man pleases the mighty.

(28) He who cultivates his land raises high his heap. He who pleases
20 the mighty takes vengeance for injustice. (29) Gifts and bribery blind the eyes of the wise; like a bit in the mouth they reject rebuke. (30) When, then, wisdom is concealed and the treasure hidden, what profit will there be in the two of them? (31) The man who conceals his ignorance is better than the one who conceals his wisdom.

25   ## ON FLEEING FROM SIN   XXI

(1) My son, if you sin, do not do so again; rather pray and beg for forgiveness for your previous sins. (2) Flee from sin as you would flee from before a serpent, for if you draw near it, it will bite you. Its fangs are like the fangs of a lion which kill and destroy the souls of men.
30 (3) All sin and all hypocrisy are like a two edged sword; there is no

healing its wound. (4) The wasting of a term loan is from hostility and insult; thus the house of the proud man is laid waste.

OF THE SUPPLICATION OF A POOR MAN

(5) The supplication of the poor man goes from his mouth to the * f. 20 rᵒ ears of the Most High and the sentence * of His vengeance comes to 5 him quickly. (6) To hate rebuke is in the footsteps of the sinner. He who fears the Lord repents in his heart. (7) The man with a mighty tongue is recognised from afar but the intelligent man acknowledges his fault when he errs. (8) He who builds his house with another's wealth is like a man who gathers his stones in the winter. (9) The 10 company of hypocrites is gathered tow and their end is a flame of blazing fire. (10) The way of sinners is level in the rocks and its final end is a pit of hell-fire. (11) He who is master of his opinion and his thought is the one who keeps the *sunna*. Wisdom is the perfection of him who fears the Lord. (12) A man who is not clever and shrewd 15 cannot be educated and some shrewdness may have much anger. (13) The wise man increases like the deluge and his counsel is like the spring of life.

OF THE FOOL AND THE WISE MAN

(14) The belly of a fool is like a broken vessel; he neither grasps nor 20 retains any knowledge, (15) but the wise man, whenever he hears a well considered word, praises it and holds it in high esteem and adds to it; it does not, however, please the crafty man when he hears it; nay, he throws it behind his back. (16) The conversation of a fool is like a load on a journey. You will find grace on the lips of the intel- 25 * f. 20 vᵒ ligent man. * (17) The mouth of the wise and prudent man is sought in the community; those who hear fix his discourse in their hearts.

(18a) Wisdom in a fool is like a broken-down house. (19) To the stupid man education is like bonds on the feet and like manacles on the right hand. (18b) The knowledge of the stupid man is neither 30 ordered nor thought out. (20) The fool when he laughs lifts his voice in his laughter; the clever, learned man however, smiles after his toil. (21) Learning and instruction are like a golden ornament to the wise

and prudent man, like a bracelet of gold on the right arm. (22)
The fool's entrance into the house is swift but the experienced man
feels shame at meeting the face of his fellow. (23) The stupid fool
looks from the door into the house, but the educated man stands
5 quietly outside. (24) He who listens at the door is a most hapless,
stupid man. It pains the wise man when he is shamed.

(25) Strangers converse with their lips but the discourse of learned,
intelligent men is weighed in the balance. (26) The heart of the ignorant fool is in his mouth; the mouths of the wise are in their hearts.

10   OF THE UNBELIEVER, THE SLANDERER,
                 AND THE INCOMPETENT

(27) The unbeliever, when he curses Satan, curses only himself. (28)
The slanderous man * defiles only himself and will be hated wher-   * f. 21 r⁰
ever he lives. (1) An incompetent man has been likened to a rejected,   **XXII**
15 cast off stone; every one blushes at his dishonor. (2) The incompetent
man has also been likened to a ball of dung that any one who picks
up will brush off his hands. (3) A father's disgrace is from a stupid,
foolish child and from a daughter when she is wanting. (4) The
prudent daughter inherits her husband but she who shames her hus-
20 band and disgraces him (5) is a disgrace to her mother and her husband and they will both despise her and hold her in contempt.

          OF AMUSEMENT AND CHASTISEMENT AND THE FOOL

(6) Amusement is not proper in the time of mourning; chastisement,
however, and instruction are desirable in all times of wisdom. (9) He
25 who teaches a fool is like him who glues a piece of pottery and like
him who awakens sleepers from deep, heavy sleep; (10) so also is he
who converses with a fool and at the end says « What is this ? ».

(11) Weep over the dead, for the light has been taken away, and
weep also over the stupid fool, for prudence and understanding have
30 been taken away. Weeping over the dead is an especially gentle
sighing, for he has come to rest and has found repose; but life for the

fool is worse than death. (12) Mourning for the dead is for seven days; but for the fool and the unbeliever, it is for all the days of their life. * f. 21 vo (13) So do not talk much * with a foolish man and do not go off to an unintelligent man, but rather keep away from him lest you have toil and grief and lest you be defiled when he brushes himself off. If 5 you leave him you will find peace.

(14) What can be heavier than lead and what is a fool called save a fool? (15) To carry sand and salt and a lump of iron is easier than to bear a stupid, foolish man.

(16) As the course of wood is bound to the structure so that when 10 it is struck by an earthquake it does not collapse, thus the firm, stead-fast heart does not tremble in the time of reflecting its counsel. (17) The heart which is firm and steadfast in its consideration of comprehen-sion and understanding is like sand that, polished, is plastered to a plaster wall. (18) Just as vine-props cannot stand firm against the 15 blowing of the wind when they are in an elevated place, so also is the cowardly, base heart in the reflection of a foolish man : it cannot stand firm in the face of any fear or fright.

OF A FRIEND

(19) He who rubs his eye brings tears to it and he who moves his 20 heart manifests understanding. (20) He who throws a stone at a bird scares it away and he who reviles his friend destroys his friend-ship. (21) If you draw your sword against your friend, do not despair * f. 22 ro of him, for he will turn back to you. * (22) If you open your mouth against your friend do not fear him or be afraid of him, for there will 25 be remonstrance and reconciliation, save in the case of your reviling him and lording it over him and your revealing his secret and your charging him with treachery and scheming, because for all these traits any friend will flee and will depart from you. (23) So acquire trust with your friend and your fellow in his poverty, so that you may 30 rejoice with him in his wealth; stand fast by him in his moment of sorrow and grief, that you may be an inheritor with him in his inherit-ance. (24) Flame and smoke arise from fire; bloodshed arises from insult. (25) Further, I am not ashamed to give asylum to my friend and I will not hide myself from his face, (26) not even if I suffer hard- 35

ship and tribulation on account of his misdeed; let everyone, therefore,
who hears this keep it in mind.

OF PRAYER TO THE LORD

(27) Who, then, will set me a guard over my mouth and who will set
me upon my lips the seal of a clever people, so that I shall not slip
or fall on account of it and so that my tongue will not destroy me? (1) **XXIII**
O Lord, the Father and master of my life, do not bring me to ruin and
do not abandon me to their counsel; do not leave me to slip and to
fall among them. (2) Who will place discipline upon my understanding
and my thought and who will put the instruction of wisdom over my
heart, that they may not eulogize me for my stupidity and my ignorance * and their sins not be forgiven them (3) and that my ignor-   * f. 22 v°
ance and stupidity may not increase and my sins be multiplied so
that I fall before my opponents who dispute with me and my enemy
rejoice over me? (4) O my Lord and God of my life, do not put me
vain pleasure in my eye (5) but rather, dispel passion from me. (6)
May neither the pleasure of the belly nor sexual passion overtake me.
Do not surrender me to a shameless soul.

OF THE FREQUENT USE OF GOD'S NAME
AND OF SWEARING OATHS

(7) Listen, my son, to my instruction and the teaching of my mouth
for he who keeps it will not go astray; (8) rather, it will remain
upon his lips. The calumniator and the haughty will doubt it. (9) Do
not accustom your mouth to swearing and do not make a habit of
frequently using the name of the Holy, (10) for just as the slave who
is perpetually chastized is not reduced by a blow, so also he who
swears and names God perpetually, in constant use, will not be purified
or cleansed of sin. (11) He who makes many oaths will be full of sin
and severe chastisement will not leave his house. If he does evil his
sin will be upon him and if he violates his oath and acts treacherously
he has sinned twice. He will not be found just if he swears falsely but
rather his house shall be filled with misfortunes. (12) A word may be

equal to death; may it never be found in the inheritance of Jacob.
The believers keep themselves far removed from all these things *
and will never wallow in their sins. (13) Do not, then, accustom your
mouth to silly talk, for sin arises from it. (14) Remember your father
and your mother. When you sit among high officials, do not act ₅
badly towards them so as to make a fool of yourself because of the
habit you have formed and wish you had never been born and curse
the day on which you were born; (15) for he who forms a habit of
abusive talk will not be educated in all the days of his life.

OF HARLOTRY AND SIN   ₁₀

(16) Sin is increased through two vices and wrath comes down on
account of the third vice. The first vice : when the soul is enflamed
like a blazing fire; it will not be extinguished until it dies out. The
second vice : when a man gives his body to harlotry; he will not cease
until his fire is enkindled. (17) The third vice : all food is pleasurable ₁₅
to the fornicator and he will not desist from it until he dies. (18) When
a man leaves his bed and betrays it, he says within himself, « Who can
see me ? Darkness encloses me. The walls surround me; no one can
see me, so whom should I fear ? The Most High will not remember my
sins; (19) I fear only the eyes of men. » He does not know that the ₂₀
eyes of the Lord are * myriads of myriads of times more brilliant
and more shining than the sun, seeing all the ways of men and search-
ing out and perceiving the most distant, hidden, and concealed regions.
(20) Just as He knows all things before He creates them, thus it is
also after He has finished with them. (21) This man has not reflected ₂₅
on the fact that he will be seized, caught and vengeance taken on him
in the public markets of the city.

(22) So also the woman who leaves her husband and raises him up
an heir from another has three vices; (23) the first vice is that she
has rebelled against the *sunna* of the Most High and betrayed it; the ₃₀
second vice is that she has sinned against her husband; the third vice
is that she has committed adultery and acted treacherously and has
produced herself children by another besides her husband. (24) She
will be openly disgraced in the community and they will shun her
children, (25) since her children will not strike roots or foundations and ₃₅

her branches will not bear fruit. (27) May, then, those who remain
after them know that there is nothing more virtuous than to fear the
Lord and nothing sweeter and more pleasant than to keep God's commandments.

OF WISDOM   XXIV

(1) Wisdom glorifies herself and boasts in the midst of her people.
(2) She opens her mouth in the assembly of the Most High [...] (3)
[...] [1] and I covered the earth like the clouds of mist. (4) I halted and
found shelter * on high and the throne of my *minbar* was set on the   * f. 24 r°
pillar of the clouds. (5) Alone I encompassed the circuit of the sky and
walked in the bottom of the deep (6) and upon the waves of the sea
and through the whole earth. I acquired possesions among every people
and tribe (7) and with all this I sought repose and said, « In whose
inheritance shall I pass the night ? ». (8) Then, at that moment, the
Creator of all commanded me; He who created me fixed my abode
and said to me, « Stay and find shelter among the people of Jacob and
make your inheritance among the people of Israel. » (9) Before eternity,
from the very beginning, He created me and unto eternity I shall
not be wanting. (10) I served before Him in the dwelling of His
purity and I became settled in Sion. (11) He established me in the
cherished city and my authority came to be in the Holy City. (12) I
then struck my roots in the noble, cherished nation and in the portion
of God and His heritage. (13) I grew tall like the cypress that is in
Lebanon and like the cedar that is on Mount Hermon (14) and like
the date palms that are in Gilgal; I became like the rose arbor that
is in Jerico and like the beautiful olive tree that is in the desert. Then,
I grew yet taller, like the plane tree; (15) I became like cinnamon *
and like aspalathus and my scent difused itself like choice myrrh,
like galbanum and aromatic unguents and storax and like the perfume
of olibanum in a tent. (16) I spread my branches and my boughs like
the terebinth; my branches are nobility and glory. (17) I brought
forth the growth of goodness like a vine; and my plant and my flower
are the fruit of nobility and glory und wealth. (19) So, draw near to
me then, o you who desire me, and be filled with my fruits, (20) for

---

[1] 2a-3b >, homoiotel. العلى.

rememberance of me is better than sweet honey and my heritage is
better than honey comb. (21) Those who eat me still hunger and those
who drink me still thirst; (22) whoever obeys me will not be shamed
and those who use me will not sin.

OF THE CODEX OF THE COVENANT OF GOD, 5
THE MOST HIGH

(23) These things are the codex of the covenant of God, the Most
High, the beacon to which Moses commanded us and the heritage
of the communities of the people of Jacob. (25) It is that which gives
satiety of wisdom, like the Nile and like the Tigris in the days of 10
planting. (26) It is that which gives abundance of understanding and
ease of life [2] like the Euphrates and like the Jordan in the days of
harvesting. (27) It is that which manifests instruction like light and
like Gihon in the days of the vintage. (28) The first did not perfect
* f. 25 rº the understanding and knowledge of it * nor did the last investigate 15
it fully, (29) since its thought is more than the sea and its counsel
more than the great deep. (30) But I, however, am like one who digs
a channel from a river; like a surveyor I went out of the garden (31)
and I said, « I will water my garden and irrigate my bed, » and my
irrigation channel became a river and my river became a sea; (32) and 20
I began to make instruction shine bright as the dawn and to make it
manifest to the ends of the earth (33) and to pour forth teaching
like prophecy and to pass it on to endless generations. (34) So, consider
this, since I have not labored and worked and toiled for myself alone,
but rather for everyone who seeks it.   25

XXV   OF GOOD AND EVIL MORAL DISPOSITION

(1) Then, I adorned myself and became comely and beautiful
before God and men with three dispositions : the first disposition
is the unanimity of brothers, one with another; the second disposition

---

[2] Cf. note on الله‌عة in *Index of Correspondences*.

is the love of comrades in God; the third disposition is the mutual understanding of a man and his wife, the one for the other.

(2) My soul has come to hate some dispositions and to be strongly
disgusted at them; the first disposition : when a poor man is proud; the
5 second disposition : when a rich man is a liar; the third disposition :
when an old man is lecherous, lacking in understanding and wit; (3)
for if, old man, * you were not trained in your childhood and * f. 25 v⁰
youth, how shall you find wisdom in your old age?

OF THE MATURE AND THEIR WISDOM

10 (4) How becoming, then, is judgement to white hairs and how
becoming is counsel and advice to old men; (5) how becoming is
wisdom to mature men and how becoming is thought and considered
opinion to men of distinction. (6) The crown of mature men is the
multitude of experiences and their boast is the fear of the Lord.
15 (7) Then, in thought and opinion I praise and bless nine things
while the tenth is upon my tongue and I shall inform you of it. The first :
when a man delights in his children; the second : when a man beholds
the downfall of his enemies within his own lifetime; (8) the third :
he who lives with a wise woman; blessed is he; the fourth : he who
20 has not slipped because of his tongue; the fifth : he who has not
served one who is unworthy; (9) the sixth : he who achieves understanding and prudence; blessed is he; the seventh : he who tells his
tale to attentive ears; (10) the bountiful eighth : he who has found
wisdom; the surpassing ninth : he who fears the Lord; (11) the tenth :
25 it is the dread of God that surpasses everything; there is none com-
parable to him who clings to it.

OF HEARTACHE AND AN EVIL WOMAN

(13) Then, any pain rather than heartache; any trouble rather than
the trouble of an evil woman; * (14) any gloating rather than the * f. 26 r⁰
30 gloating of those who hate; any vengeance rather than the vengeance
of enemies. (15) There is no head worse or more vile than the head of
a serpent and there is no anger more violent than the anger of an
enemy.

(16) Indeed, I should rather live with a lion or a dragon rather than live with an evil woman. (17) The badness of an evil woman alters the appearance of her face and makes her face dark as the face of a bear. (18) Whenever her husband reclines with his companions and hears something of her, he heaves a bitter sigh. (19) Any trouble is 5 less than the trouble of an evil woman. She falls to the lot of the sinner. (20) As sand encumbers the feet of an elderly man, so is a talkative woman to a mild, gentle man. (21) So, do not fall on account of an evil woman's beauty, (22) for she is wrath, slander and great disgrace. An evil woman, whenever she nags her husband, (23) humiliates his 10 heart and distorts his countenance and pains his heart with her feeble hands and shriveled knees. No one says to her husband on her account, « Blessed are you ». (24) The first sin came to be through a woman and we shall all die on account of her. (25) So give water no outlet nor an evil woman freedom over you. (26) If she will not put herself under 15 your authority, cut her off from your flesh.

XXVI   OF A RIGHTEOUS WOMAN

(1) Blessed is the man who has dominance over a righteous woman,
* f. 26 v° for he has had the number of his days doubled. * (2) A staid, agile, active woman causes her husband's heart to rejoice; she perfects his 20 life in peace. (3) A righteous woman is a righteous portion and a gift from the Lord to those who fear Him. (4) Both the rich man and the poor man should be of upright heart and of bright, cheerful countenance on all occasions.

OF THE FOUR FACES   25

(5) My heart has dreaded three faces and the fourth face I have feared. The first face : a group of citizens who have divided into factions; the second face : false witness, for it is equal to death; (6) the third face : the heartache of a wailing woman who has become jealous of another woman; the fourth face : a tongue-lashing, for it is 30 common to the worst of men and the jealousy of a woman.

OF AN ADULTEROUS, DRUNKEN WOMAN

(7) An adulterous woman is like setting a pair of oxen in motion and who who gets her is like him who lays hold of a scorpion. (8) A drunken woman is a great affliction; she will never hide and conceal her shame. (9) A woman's harlotry can be recognized in the look of her eyes and in the movement of her eyelashes. (10) If, then, you have a heastrong, immoral daughter, keep strict watch over her so that she will not find an opportunity to give herself free rein.

(11) Then, beware of him who does not divert his eyes from you and do not be surprised if he wrongs you, * (12) for he will open * f. 27 r° his mouth to you like a thirsty traveler who drinks from any water that is near him and will make a place for you before every tent-peg and will open his quiver against you in front of the arrow.

OF A WISE, QUIET WOMAN

(13) A wise woman brings joy to her husband with her goodness and softens his bones with her wisdom and her understanding. (14) A quiet woman is a trust, a gift from the Lord. There is no equivalent to, and no substitute for, a disciplined soul (15). A woman who is modest and pious is a blessing upon a blessing; nothing can measure her worth in a balance or be equal to her. (16) The sun rises in the Lord's heights; such is the beauty of a righteous woman in this world in her house, (17) like the lamp that shines on a holy lampstand and like the beauty of the look of a face of balanced proportions, (18) like pillars of gold upon silver bases, like graceful feet upon firm heels.

OF THREE THINGS

(28) At two things my heart is distressed and at the third I am filled with anger. The first : at a warrior who is distitute at the end of his life; the second : at learned men who come to be contemtuously rejected; the third : at a man who passes from righteousness to sin; The Lord will prepare His sword for him.

OF THE MERCHANT AND THE WINE-SELLER *

(29) With difficulty will a merchant avoid doing injustice and a
XXVII wine-seller will not be held free of sin. (1) Many have been charged
with sin because of excessive spending and the greedy man who
desires increase <averts> his eye. (2) As a peg is inserted between ₅
the cracks of a rock, thus is sin rubbed between buying and selling.
(3) If a man does not master himself in fear of the Lord, his house
soon will quickly be laid waste.

OF TESTING A MAN AND HIS WORDS

(4) As the dung remains when the sieve is shaken, thus a man is ₁₀
rejected by the movement of his talk. (5) As an earthen vessel is
tested in the kiln, thus a man is tested in his thought and his talk. (6)
As a well cultivated tree shows its fruit, thus a man's speech shows the
care of his heart. (7) So, do not praise a man before letting him speak,
since a man is tested by his speech alone.   ₁₅

OF SEEKING TRUTH AND JUSTICE

(8) If you seek truth and justice you will attain it and you will
put it on like a robe of glory. (9) Birds gather with their own kind and
truth comes to those who act by it. (10) As the lion lurks for the prey,
so does sin lurk for those who work evil. (11) The talk of the believer ₂₀
* f. 28 r° is at all times in wisdom but the stupid, foolish man * changes like
<the moon>.

OF THE LEARNED AND THE IGNORANT

(12) Beware of ignorant, stupid men for a time and be among the
learned constantly, (13) for the conversation of stupid men is disgust ₂₅
and their laughter is conducive to sin. (14) The discourse of those
who swear many oaths makes one's hair stand on end and their clamor
stops up one's ears. (15) The clamor of the proud, however, spills
blood and their contention is foul to hear.

OF ONE WHO DIVULGES A SECRET

(16) He who divulges a secret destroys his trust and cannot find himself a friend; (17) so, hold fast to your friend and perpetuate your trust with him and if you divulge his secret do not look for his track, 5 (18) because as a man destroys his enemy, so does he destroy the bond of friendship with his fellow when he divulges his secret. (19) Like the bird which you have released from your hand, thus have you released your friend; (20) so, do not seek him at all, for he has stationed himself far away from you and has fled from you like the gazelle from 10 the snares. (21) There is bandaging and medication for a wound and there is rebuke for an insult, but there is no rebuking one who divulges secrets.

OF ONE WHO WINKS HIS EYE

(22) He who winks his eye works evil; no one at all can keep it 15 away from him, (23) for before your eyes he sweetens the speech of his mouth and shows pleasure at your speech; thereafter he contorts his mouth and casts doubt on your speech. * (24) [Th]is man I have * f. 28 v° hated exceedingly and I have not resembled him; the Lord hates him too. (25) He who throws a stone up high only throws it upon 20 his own head; wounds are multiplied by a treacherous sinful blow. (26) He who digs a pit will fall into it and he who sets up a snare will be caught by it. (27) He who works evil, it shall be upon him without his knowing whence it came to him. (28) The proud scoff and revile while vengeance lurks for them like a lion. (29) Those who rejoice 25 at the fall of the believers will perish in the trap; grief will destroy them before death.

OF RANCOR

(30) Rancor and wrath are hateful and it is the sinful man who clings to them. (1) He who takes vengeance on his fellow shall find XXVIII 30 vengeance with the Lord; he makes firm his own sins; (2) so forgive your fellow his injustice and then, whenever you make humble entreaty, your sins will be forgiven. (3) If, in anger, a man hold rancor against

a man how shall he seek healing from the Lord? (4) If he have not
mercy towards a man like himself, how shall he long for the Lord on
account of his own sins? (5) If he nourish rancor, being himself of
flesh, who is there who will forgive him his sins? (6) Remember,
therefore, your end and refrain from enmity; remember death and 5
change of fortune and keep the commandments. (7) Remember the
* f. 29 r⁰ commandments * and do not hold rancor against your fellow. Remember the covenant of the Most High and overlook the offense of your
fellow.

OF AVOIDING STRIFE   10

(8) Keep away from strife so as to diminish your sins, for the wrath-
ful man enkindles strife. (9) The sinful man raises strife between
brothers; between those who are at peace he stirs up denouncement
and division. (10) The blazing of fire is in proportion to the amount
of its heat; a man's anger is proportionate to his strength and his 15
wrath rises in proportion to his wealth. (11) Long lasting contention
enkindles fire and long lasting strife causes bloodshed, (12) since,
if you blow upon a spark, it will blaze up and if you spit on it it will die
out and both things come forth from your mouth.

OF THE SLANDERER AND THE TWO-TONGUED   20

(13) Cursed be the slanderer and the two-tongued, for they have
destroyed many who were at peace. (14) The slandering tongue has
aroused many and has transferred them and displaced them from
nation to nation; it has destroyed walled cities and laid waste the
houses of the mighty. (15) The slandering tongue has driven hearty 25
women far away and deprived them of their children and their wealth.
(16) He who possesses it will find no rest; he will not dwell in peace
and ease. (17) A wound comes from the blow of a whip but the blow
of the tongue shatters the bones. (18) They have fallen by the points
* f. 29 v⁰ of swords but they are not like * those who have fallen by the tongue. 30
(19) Blessed, then, is he who is shielded against it and he who has
not crossed over into its anger and has not borne its yoke and he who
has not been bound in its fetters, (20) because its yoke is a yoke of

iron and its fetters are fetters of bronze; (21) its death is a shameful
death and its hell-fire is the hell-fire of perdition forever. (22) The
believers do not cling to it and are not burned in its flame. (23) Those
who forsake the Lord shall fall into it and it will blaze in them and not
5 be quenched; rather, it will be set upon them like a lion and will seize
them like a panther. (24) Look, then, and fence your house round
with thorns; bind up your silver and your gold; (25) give restraint
and measure to your speech and set a gate and a bar over your mouth.
(26) Beware lest you fall on account of it or fall before him who lies
10 in wait for you.

OF LENDING MONEY WITH MERCY   XXIX

(1) The one who performs an act of mercy lends to his kinsman
and he who gives freely with his hand according to his ability
is the one who keeps the commandments. (2) So, lend to your kinsman
15 in the time of his need and bestow your gift on your kinsman in its
time, (4) for many consider a loan as something found and vex and
sadden him who helped them (5) to the point that he takes them by
the hands and kisses them. When they want their neighbor's wealth *   * f. 30 r⁰
they address him with sadness and flattery, but when his payment
20 becomes due they put it off a year and speak to him in annoyance and
complain of the time. (6) If they can, they remit him half under
pressure and reckon it against him as something found. Otherwise,
they have deprived him of his wealth and gratuitously gained themselves an enemy. Then they curse him and revile him instead of honor-
25 ing him. (7) Many have, on this account, refused many people for
fear of their evil and for fear of being deprived of their wealth to no
purpose. (8) But lengthen your forebearance for the man who is poor
and do not withold yourself from almsgiving. (9) Strengthen the
unfortunate man for the commandment's sake and do not send him
30 off empty, destitute as he is. (10) Indeed, give away silver on behalf
of your brother and your friend. (11) Build your fortune according
to the commandments of the Most High and it will benefit you more
than your amassing gold. (12) Store up alms in your cellars for it
will save you from every evil (13) and instead of want it will be for
35 you strength and, instead of profit, a support and before you it will
fight off your enemies from you.

OF GOING SURETY

(14) The righteous man is he who goes surety for his fellow. The one who is shameless rejects him who has gone surety for him; (15) so, do not forget the generosity of him who has gone surety for you, for he has given of himself on your behalf. (16) The righteous surety 5 * f. 30 v° keeps his pledge to the sinner. * (17) He, however, who rejects and grieves the one who has saved him has no goodness. (18) Going surety has destroyed many independant men and has shaken them like the swell of the sea; it has vanquished strong, powerful men and they erred and went to excess among strange peoples. (19) The sinful 10 man, when he has to go surety, seeks compensation and has to pay a penalty. (20) So, strengthen your kinsman and your fellow, so far as you are able, and watch out for yourself lest you fall.

OF HUMAN LIFE AND MOVING FROM PLACE TO PLACE

(21) The first of man's life is of bread and water and clothing and in 15 the house that conceals and covers nakedness and shame. (22) Better a papuer's means beneath a wooden roof than pleasant foods in strange parts; (23) so let your joy be one with what is great and what is small. (24) The evil life is to move from house to house and to dwell in rented lodging; you can neither dwell in peace nor open your mouth. 20 (25) No, you will offer hospitality and give drink without praise when the master of the house says to you, (26) « Get up, lodger, and prepare me the table and embelish it; give me to eat what you have in your hands; (27) be gone, lodger, from the house, for my brother has come to me as my guest and I have need of the house. » (28) How oppressive 25 it is for an intelligent man to be scolded for a matter of lodgings and * f. 31 r° to be rebuked by a creditor. *

XXX   OF TRAINING ONE'S SON

(1) He who loves his son prolongs his punishment so that he may rejoice in him at the end. (2) He who trains his son shall rejoice in 30 him and shall boast of him among his acquaintences. (3) He who

instructs his son will excite the envy of his enemy and will rejoice in
him and find delight in the presence of his brethren. (4) When his
father dies it is as if he had not died, since he has left behind him one
like himself. (5) He beheld him during his life and rejoiced and was
5 not grieved at his dying, (6) since he has left behind him some one
to take vengeance upon his enemies and some one to repay and reward
his brethren with goodness. (7) He will bind his wounds from their
sons and his breast will tremble at their every sound.

(8) A horse, when it is not broken, goes out stubornly and a lax son,
10 when he has not been trained, goes out of the house. (9) If you take
him to yourself, he will make a fool of you and if you play with him, he
will grieve you. (10) Do not laugh with him lest you be grieved and
gnash your teeth in the end. (11) Do not give him any authority in
his youth, (12) but rather break his ribs while he is still a child, lest he
15 be hardened to disobey you. (13) Discipline your son and put him to
work, lest you fall in his disgrace.

OF GOOD HEALTH

(14) The poor man who is in good health and recovered is better
than the rich man who is afflicted in his body. (15) Health and sound-
20 ness of body are better than all wealth; a body which is always healthy
is better than countless wealth. * (16) There is no wealth better * f. 31 v°
than the health of the body and there is no joy greater than the joy
of the heart. (17) Death is preferable to a bitter life and enduring
illness.
25 (18) Good things in a closed mouth are like foods placed in a grave.
(21) So, do not grieve yourself in your counsel, (22) for the heart's
cheer is life to a man and a man's joy lengthens his life. (23) Grant
your soul its desire and console your heart; put sadness far away
from you, for sadness has killed many and there is neither profit nor
30 benefit in it. (24) Envy and anger diminish one's days and care brings
on gray hair before its time.

OF GOOD COUNSEL

(25) Then, like one who seeks the path of the reapers I have sought

the blessing of the Lord and I came upon it and filled a press like the reaper. (26) I did not toil and strive for myself alone but for every one who seeks training. (27) So listen to me, you, the mighty of the nation, and attend to me, you, the foremost of the community, (28) son, wife, brother, and friend; give no one authority over you during 5 your life and do not hand your wealth over to anyone other than your-self, lest you repent and have to go seek it, (29) as long as you live and there is spirit in you. Do not prefer any one over your self, (30) for it is better for your sons that they have need of you than that you * f. 32 r⁰ look at what is in their hands. * (31) Be perfect in all your actions and 10 place no defect in your glory (32) all the days of your life.

OF SLAVES

(33) Work a slave and feed him and train him, (34) for if you work your slave, you will find rest and if you relax your hands on him, he will seek manumission. (35) Just as the yoke and bonds cause the 15 neck to bend so does torture and exemplary punishment to the slave who does evil; (36) so put him to work lest he become unproductive, (37) for idleness has procured much evil. (38) Keep him at work as befits him and, if he does not obey you, increase the weight of his chains. 20

XXXI   OF DREAMS

(1) Dreams put stupid people to flight. (2) Like one who seeks after a shadow and the wind, thus is he who accepts dreams. (3) The visions of dreams are similar to one another as a face resembles a face. (4) Who, then, is able to become clean and pure of defilement or who 25 accepts the truth from a liar? (5) Dreams and fortunes are vain and the heart rejoices in them like her who gives birth to a child (6) unless they are sent intentionally by the Most High. So, do not let your heart incline towards them, (7) for dreams have misled many and they have fallen because they trusted in them. 30

(8) The *sunna* is perfect, without lie and wisdom is perfect in the mouths of the believers, (15) since their trust is in Him who saved * f. 32 v⁰ them. * (16) He who fears the Lord is afraid of nothing: he does not

become faint, for <his trust> is in Him. (17) Blessed is the soul
that fears the Lord (18) and the one who adopts the fear of the Lord
and keeps it. (19) The eyes of the Lord are upon those who love Him
with devotion, like a mighty defense and a strong protection and like
5 a cover that hides them from the heat and the noonday He will guard
them from harm and assist them when they fall, (20) lift up their
souls and enlighten their eyes, and give them healing and life and
blessing.

OF THE POOR AND THE HIRED MAN

10   (25) The life of a poor man consists in the bread that he begs and
he who deprives him of it is like one who sheds blood. (26) The one
who kills his fellow is he who takes his sustenance away from him
against his will. (27) He who deprives the hired man of his wages is
like one who sheds blood. (28) When one builds and one tears down,
15 what is the use of toil and much labor? (29) When one prays and the
other curses, to the voice of which of these two will the Lord, the
Master, listen? (30) When a man makes his ablution and purifies
himself from contact with a corpse and then touches it again, what
benefit has he in that bath? (31) Such is the man who will fast on
20 account of his sins and they go out and commit them again. Who will
answer his prayer and what profit is there in his humbling himself?   **XXXII**
     (5) The good pleasure of God * is to keep far distant from sins and * f. 33 r⁰
His forgiveness is to keep far distant from injustice, (6) so do not
show yourself before the Lord empty, (10) but rather praise the Lord
25 with a righteous eye and do not stint the gift of your hand. (11) Make
your countenance radiant and joyful with every gift you give; (12)
give to the Most High as He has given, with a righteous eye according
to what your hands find, (13) for the Lord will repay you and reward
you sevenfold. (15) The Lord is judge, governor, and there is no
30 partiality with Him. (16) He does not show preference to men of
prestige against the poor, but rather He hears the prayer of the man
who is oppressed. (17) He is not heedless of the entreaty of orphans
nor of the widow, if she speaks and calls to Him. (18) The tears of
the widow run down her cheek (19) and her plea is against the one who
35 made them flow. (21) The prayer of the poor man rises above the

clouds and it will not be consoled until it draws near and approaches and will not depart until the Most High turns His attention to it.

XXXIV   OF SITTING AT TABLE

(12) Then, if you sit at a magnificent table, do not gape at it and do not comment that what is upon it is much. (13) Reflect, rather, 5 for an evil eye is wicked and nothing was created that is more wicked than the eye, wherefore it weeps on account of every face. (14) Do not put forth your hand wherever you look and do not grieve any one on account of a bowl. (15) Rather, recognize what belongs to your kinsman out of concern for yourself and be cognisant of all things. (16) 10 * f. 33 v° Eat like the man whatever is brought and placed before you * and do not champ so that you may not become hated. (17) For the sake of good manners be the first to stop and do not take a great quantity of food lest you blunder. (18) If you sit among a large company, never be the first of them to put forth your hand, (19) for a little is sufficient 15 for a well-bred man and when he does thus he will not fall ill upon his bed.

OF REST AND EXTRAVAGANCE

(20) To lie abed in measure is health for him who does so to rise at daybreak from his sleep, his soul with him. Being in the company of 20 an extravagant man is a great effort, sleeplessness, foulness, and torture. (21) If you should be pressed to foods against your will, arise from the midst of the company and take your rest.

(22) Hear from me, my son, and do not disdain me, for in the end you will discover my discourse. Be prudent in all your discourse and 25 no illness will overtake you at all. (23) He who is cheerful and lives well invokes a blessing upon the food with his lips and the witness for him is his beauty and loyalty. (24) But the wicked man whines and becomes much annoyed over his food, and the witness against him is his wickedness and his evil conviction.   30

(25) Do not become frolicsome for drinking wine, for wine has caused many to go astray and to err. (26) Like the test of dipping a poker in the furnace, thus is wine in the hearts of the proud. (27) Wine

sustains man's life, * so drink it in moderation, sufficiency, and due * f. 34 rᵒ
measure, without excess. (31) Do not substitute wine-drinking for
your friend and your companion.

OF THE MATURE MAN AND THE YOUTH   XXXV

5   (3) Speak, o mature man, for that befits you; may your discourse
be with certainty, learning, and understanding. (4) Do not pour
forth your discourse where there should be listening nor play the
wise one with foolish judgement. (7) Do not talk, o youth; if you have
to talk, let your speaking be twice at most, if you are asked. (8) Be
10 concise and with little speaking aim at much; be like the one who
knows but is silent. (9) Do not act proudly among the great and do
not remain impassioned over whatever they may speak of, (10) for
the lightning hurries before the thunder and from him who is modest
comes grace. (11) Arise when you should and do not dally; go home
15 and do not delay. (12) Play there and do what you will; do not sin
and do not speak haughtily. (13) Bless Him, all the while, Who
created you and filled you and blessed you from His bounties, (14)
for he who fears the Lord accepts training and those who seek Him
early in the morning shall find His good-pleasure.

20 OF THOSE WHO FEAR THE LORD AND OF ADMONISHMENT

(16) Those who fear the Lord will find judgement; like a shining
light, thus their gifts will gleam. (17) The sinful man turns aside from
admonition; * he seeks judgement according to his own desire. (18) * f. 34 vᵒ
The thoughtful man [...]; the enemy does not approach him; the
25 proud man departs from him. (19) So do nothing without taking
counsel and do not tarry in the meantime. (20) Do not travel a path
on which one slips and do not fall over a rock twice. (21) Do not trust
a path in which there is no stumbling. (22) But, beware your sons.
(23) Have faith in yourself in every work you do, for thus is the keeping
30 of the commandments. (24) He who trusts in the Lord will not be
wanting. (1) Evil shall not come upon him who fears the Lord; rather, **XXXVI**
he shall be rescued and safe from tribulation.
    (4) Prepare a word and then speak it; put on training and then

reply, (5) for the guts of a fool are like a cart-wheel and his thought
is like a revolving water-wheel. (6) A rejected friend is like a trouble-
some horse that sits in the lowest place and wails.

XXXVII   OF TAKING COUNSEL

(10) Do not, then, seek the counsel of him who spies on you; indeed, ₅
hide your counsel from those who persecute you. (11) Do not consult
a woman concerning another woman, lest she become jealous of you;
do not consult a merchant concerning his business activity; do not
* f. 35 r⁰ consult a buyer concerning a sale; do not consult an envious man *
concerning the praise of anyone; do not consult the merciless concern- ₁₀
ing good moral conduct; do not consult a lazy man on a job you wish
to do; do not consult a hired man on a matter you want completed;
do not consult a useless slave on any job whatsoever. Do not refrain
altogether from consultation because of these things, (12) but rather,
make constant consultation with the man who is a believer, who you ₁₅
know keeps the commandments, whose soul is like your soul, and
who, if you sin or err, with be with you then.
(13) Remain firm in the counsel of your heart, since you have none
like it, (14) for a man's soul advises him his counsel whenever he
consults it, better than seven spies sitting in a watchtower. (15) ₂₀
Direct your desire towards the Most High in all this, in order that He
may establish your way in honesty. (16) The word is the first of every
action and before every action is consultation. (17) The heart's
concern changes (18) and from it arise four parts : good and evil and
life and death, and it is the tongue that has power over this at all times. ₂₅

OF THE CLEVER, THE EDUCATED, THE WISE

(19) A man may be clever, shrewd, and highly educated and neither
improve nor arouse his own soul (20) and may be one who shows
* f. 35 v⁰ wisdom in speech and yet be depised. * He who is like this distorts
all wisdom (21) because he is not one given a blessing from the Lord. ₃₀
(22) A man may be wise in the judgement of his soul and his fruit,
his wisdom and his understanding, is in the mouths of the believers.
(23) The wise man trains his people and his fruit, his wisdom and his

understanding, is trustworthy. (24) The wise man shall be filled with blessings and all those who look upon him shall say « Blessed are you! ». (26) He will inherit trust among his people and his name will live forever.

OF TESTING THE SOUL
AND EXTRAVAGANCE AND EXCESS

(27) So, test your soul, my son, during your lifetime; discover what is contrary to it and do not indulge it in that, (28) for all things are not suitable for it; every soul does not find pleasure in everything. (29) Do not take all foods in large quantity, (30) for illness comes from abundance of foods. Extravagance and excess lead to ruin. (31) Many have died from excessiveness and the life of those who were moderate has been long.

OF THE PHYSICIAN   XXXVIII

(1) Honor the physician for his honor is in his hands. (2a) If there is healing, it is from the Lord, the Most High. (3a) His wisdom and understanding lift up the physician's head; (2b) he receives honor from the king (3b) and the mighty wonder at him, (4) for the Lord is the one who created drugs from the earth * and the wise man does *. f 36 rº not refuse them. (5) Did not sweet water spring from the wood in order that His power might be known? (6) It is the Lord who gave men wisdom concerning them in order that they might glorify His wonders. (7) By means of them He heals them and relieves their sufferings. (8) The perfumer makes his perfume from their mixtures. There is no ending or term to the works of the Lord; nay, from them there is peace on the face of the whole earth.

OF SICKNESS

(9) So do not tarry, my son, in your illness or wait, but pray to the Lord; He will cure you. (10) Extend your hand to giving and keep far away from injustice and cleanse your heart of all sin. (12) Make a

place for the physician, for the Lord created him; may he not be far
from you, for you will have need of him, (13) since the time comes
when the sweet scent will be in their hands. (14) Physicians long for
the Lord in order that he may grant them and grace them <with>
rest and healing for the sake of their sustenance. (15) He falls at the 5
hand of the physician who has sinned before His creator.

OF THE DEAD

(16) Then, let tears flow for the dead; begin the lament like one
who has suffered a severe blow. Wrap his body in its shrowd, as fits the
situation and do not neglect his burial. (17) Weep bitterly and cry hot 10
the lament; mourn for him as befits him, one day and two, as is the
* f. 36 vᵒ custom, * and be consoled from your grief, (18) for grief sends forth
death and the heart's grief saps one's strength (19) and prolongs
misfortune.

OF HIM WHO SEEKS KNOWLEDGE

(34) He who leads his soul in the persuit of knowledge and who 15
XXXIX understands the *sunna* of the Most High and comprehends it, (1) who
seeks after the wisdom of all the ancients and is studious in the matters
of the prophets, (2) and who learns the reports of wise men and ever
and again repeats the parables and their meanings, (4) he will serve
the mighty and will appear before the foremost and will travel among 20
foreign peoples and will experience good and evil among men. (5) He
will reflect in his heart and go before dawn to the Lord Who created
him; he will entreat the Most High for his sins and open his mouth in
prayer (6) and the Almighty Lord will fill him with the spirit of understanding and he will increase and pour forth his wise discourse and 25
give thanks to the Lord in his prayer. (7) He will make straight his
counsel and his wisdom and will comprehend His mysteries (8) and
he will show forth the discipline of his teaching and will glory in the
sunna of the Lord and in His covenant. (9) Many will praise his
wisdom and it shall not be erased for ever. Memory of him will not 30
become remote and pass away but rather his name shall live for
generations of generations (10) and men will recount tales of his

wisdom and the community will praise him and tell of him. (11) If he continues to live and endures, his name will be better than a thousand names and if he dies, he shall be such. *

* f. 37 r⁰

OF KINDNESS   XL

⁵ (17) Kindness is like Paradise in blessings and mercy endures for-ever. (18) The life of the competent workman is pleasant but greater than both is he who finds a treasure. (19) Children and the city's prosperity secure the *sunna* but greater than both is the woman in whom there is no fault. (20) The heart's gladness is wine and amuse-¹⁰ ment but greater than both is the love of wisdom. (21) The city takes its pleasure with the horn and the flute but greater than both is the tongue that guides. (22) The eye's desire is joy and beauty but greater than both is the green of the crops. (23) The eye's pleasure is a friend and his companion when they meet at their appointed times but ¹⁵ greater than both is a woman with her husband. (24) Brothers and helpers in moments of grief but greater than both is mercy that saves. (25) Gold and silver make firm one's foot but greater than both is the counsel of a person of established goodness. (26) Power and wealth lift up the heart but greater than both is the fear of the Lord; there ²⁰ is no deficiency in the fear of the Lord and with it no help need be sought.

OF A LIFE OF BEGGING

(28) So, do not lead a life of begging, my son, for it is better for you that you die and not beg. (29) The man who gazes at another's table ²⁵ does not reflect on the sustenance of his life; * rather, he disgraces his soul and casts shame on it with a stranger's foods; but the prudent, well-bred man restrains himself in this. (30) Begging is pleasant in the mouth of an ignorant man but in his belly it is a burning fire.

* f. 37 v⁰

OF DEATH, BITTER AND GOOD   XLI

³⁰ (1) O death, how bitter is the rememberance of you to the man who

is secure in his wealth, who is blessed in all things, worried about nothing, who is able to take food. (2) O death, how good is your sentence to the man who is poor, who begs for his food, who is weak, and to the old man, worn out, who is worried about everything, rejected, forsaken, who has gone astray in his forebearance. (3) Do 5 not fear the sentence of death, but rather think of those who were before and [who will be] after you, (4) for this sentence is from the Lord upon each and every one. Do not, then, contend with good-pleasure of the Most High. If you live ten, a hundred, or a thousand years, in hell-fire there is no reproaching life.   10

OF A GOOD NAME, GOOD TRAINING, AND SHAME

(12) Then, consider a good name so that it may remain yours, better for you than thousands of great treasures of gold. (13) A good life consists in the sum of days but a good name lasts forever; (14) so, hold to your good training, my children, in peace. When wisdom is hidden 15 * f. 38 rᵒ and a treasure concealed, * what benefit is there in the two of them? (15) To hide his stupidity and ignorance is better for a man than that he hide and conceal his wisdom. (16) Be shamed and strive to carry out my word, for it is not good for one to keep every kind of shame and not to test all that belongs to trust.   20

(17) However, be ashamed to commit adultery with father or mother; be ashamed to lie to a man of prestige and power; (18) be ashamed to sin before a judge or minister; be ashamed to do evil before the community and the people; be ashamed to do injustice to an associate and friend; (19) be ashamed to commit theft in the 25 place, so that you may dwell there; be ashamed for God's truth and His covenant; be ashamed to prop your elbow on bread; be ashamed of foolishly taking and giving; (20) be ashamed of keeping silence towards those who greet you; be ashamed of looking at a woman not one of your own women; (21) be ashamed of turning your faces from 30 your kinsmen; be ashamed of exausting your portion or of giving it away; be ashamed of turning about to look at a woman with her husband (22) and of trafficking with her slave-girl and of visiting her bed; be ashamed to revile your friend with a word; be ashamed of **XLII** reviling after giving a gift (1) and of making qualifications in listening 35

to a word and of divulging a secret, unrevealed conversation. Be modest
and truthful * and you shall find favor with every man.   * f. 38 v°

OF RELINQUISHING SHAME

Attend, my son, that you be not ashamed of these things: do not
be ashamed not to enter into something in which one will sin (2)
5 according to what is in the *sunna* of the Most High and His covenant,
nor of a judgement in which you do not declare the unbeliever to be
innocent, (3) nor of one who is justly your associate or companion
on a journey, nor of giving an inheritance to its rightful possessors, (4)
nor of testing the measure and the scales, nor of acquiring little and
10 much, (5) nor of diversified dealing with merchants, nor of training
children much, nor, when you have a wicked slave, of drawing blood
from his flanks, (6) nor of putting a seal on an evil woman by binding,
nor of locking up where there are many hands, (7) — let all that you
give or take be counted and weighed — nor or taking and receiving
15 each thing with a written contract, (8) nor of disciplining and rebuking
a lackbrain, stupid ignoramus, nor to call to account an old man, at the
last of his age, for adultery, and you will be learned, perspicatious,
experienced in everything, more than every living person.

(33) Praise the Lord who created all things,   XLIII
20   Who gives wisdom to the believers.

Finished and complete is the Wisdom of Ibn Sirach, the wise
in good training for those who need good training, through
the power of Christ, Our Lord, to Whom be praise for all ages.
                    Amen.

CONTENTS